Theodore F. Wright

Life Eternal

Theodore F. Wright
Life Eternal
ISBN/EAN: 9783337119430
Printed in Europe, USA, Canada, Australia, Japan
Cover: Foto ©Lupo / pixelio.de

More available books at **www.hansebooks.com**

"He that loveth his life shall lose it, and he that hateth his life in this world shall keep it unto life eternal."—JOHN xii. 25.

BY
THEODORE F. WRIGHT.

BOSTON:
MASSACHUSETTS NEW-CHURCH UNION,
169 TREMONT STREET.
1885.

CONTENTS.

	PAGE
BEYOND THE GRAVE	7
MAN A SPIRIT	21
DEATH	37
THE LORD'S EXAMPLE IN DEATH	55
RESURRECTION	67
THE LORD'S RESURRECTION	82
REUNION ON HIGH	96
THE BIBLE IN HEAVEN	111
THE HEAVENWARD CALL	125
THE HEAVENLY PREPARATION	139
IN AFFLICTION	154
AFTER AFFLICTION	169

PREFACE.

IN complying with a wish, expressed both within and without the society of the New Church, which he serves, that certain discourses, prepared at various times for the purpose of giving the teachings of the Holy Word and of fair reasoning on the subject of the future life, might be placed within the reach of those who have known bereavement or who may for other reasons be led to take near views of death, the author would say that these sermons are neither so closely connected as to form an argument, nor so nicely discriminated as to avoid repetition, and that they are sent forth only in the hope that some hearts may find therein "comfortable words"; may be led to doubt that

> "Death
> Grinned horrible a ghastly smile, to hear
> His famine should be filled;"

and to believe that

> "Death is another life. We bow our heads
> At going out, we think, and enter straight
> Another golden chamber of the king's,
> Larger than this we leave, and lovelier."

BRIDGEWATER, Mass.,
Feb., 1885.

BEYOND THE GRAVE.

"As the angels of God in heaven."—MATT. xxii. 30.

THERE are three ways of looking at the life hereafter, and it is proposed to consider them a little in order to see on what basis rests the doctrine of the New Church. How to prepare for the future life is obviously a question of the greatest importance, but it is equally evident that according to the idea we have of that other life will be our preparation. Moreover, it must be plain that if all men could be made to see clearly the nature of this after life, a new and most powerful motive would be added to those which lead them to contend with evil and do what is right. If the idea of the future existence be vague, the preparation must be made in doubt. If the thought be that the future life is itself a matter of doubt, then no direct preparation whatever can be made for it.

If its reality and the nature of its existence be well known, then, like a mariner who sees before him the harbor for which he steers, one may go on, not only hopefully, but securely.

Of these three ideas it may be said that the first was formerly held generally, and is now widely held in the Christian Church, but with a gradual decrease of confidence, the current of popular opinion setting from it rather than towards it. A few words from the Westminster Catechism brings this view to mind. "The bodies of men after death return to dust and corruption. The souls of the righteous, being then made perfect in holiness, are received into the highest heaven, where they behold the face of God in light and glory. But the souls of the wicked are cast into hell, where they remain in torments and utter darkness. At the last day the dead shall be raised up, with the self-same bodies, and none others, which shall be united to their souls forever."

It will be seen that under this view men obtain only the boon of an unorganized existence from the time of death to the last day, when they must return to their bodies. How small the number in light must be comparatively, will be seen by what the "Shorter Catechism" says of the heathen; "They who, having never heard the Gospel, know not Christ Jesus, and believe not in him, cannot be saved, be they ever so diligent to frame their lives according to the light of nature, or the law of the religion they profess."

It is not necessary to put this statement on trial, and it is not unkind to say that it is not a good view to take. It is not the Lord's truth; it is not in the words of Scripture, and cannot be put into them; it is some man's writing, and he was, evidently, a very fallible man. This view would promote skepticism with some, and would make others cower in the sight of God, when they should be rejoicing and working. Now here is no helpful light as to what men should do in preparation for the hereafter. If not predestined, nothing can help them; if predestined, nothing can help their having the full glories of the hereafter; but those glories are to be in the "self-same body and none other." This is not an ennobling view, but its failings have been sufficiently indicated. It is clear that the motive to good in it is nothing as regards the great body of mankind who have not the Gospel, and but little more as regards those who are either doomed to everlasting torture, or to a return to the body.

This view, arising from a misunderstanding of the Scriptures, has given rise, as would be expected, to an opposite one. A very large class of people in Christendom doubt this view because it is not reasonable, and draw away from the Scriptures, which they are told give authority to this view, and seek to hold a virtuous course in life without the help of a faith in the hereafter. "George Eliot" was a leader in this party. She had no conviction of the hereafter, and but little respect for anything connected with the Christian Church, which seemed to her to be in error. She formed her life here according to what she believed to be reasonable, and lived and died unsustained by any faith in heavenly life. Another agnostic, of a lighter mental caliber, died not long ago, having given direction that his tomb should bear the inscription; "I was not, I lived, I loved, I am not." Out of nothingness he believed he came, to nothingness he was going; a hopeless, helpless view, indeed. This view also is man-made. It, too, is unscriptural, unreasonable. Received only as a dire necessity, it gives no strength to the living, no comfort to the dying. It is enough to say of it, in its cold negations, "My heart and my flesh cry out for the living God."

As to the third view, let it be said that when it came from the lips of the Lord Jesus, the situation of the faiths was much as it is now. There were two opinions standing over against each other. Pharisees on one side, and Sadducees on the other, held the same attitude with Calvinists and agnostics to-day. The Pharisee believed in predestination and election, namely, of his people to heaven, and of all others to hell. He claimed that this was scriptural, and quoted passages, the meaning of which he misunderstood. His heaven was a narrow paradise, namely, the Holy Land transformed; his hell was a burning Tophet. The Saduccean idea was negative. It denied that the Scriptures taught what the Pharisees believed. It stopped there, not being able to build a better faith, just as modern Sudducceism stops. The third view then is the third view now. The third view then was from a better interpretation of the Scriptures; it is so now; and it is the same view brought back after being lost, and made bright with the effulgence of the new age of Christianity.

What is this view? When the Lord went up into the mountain and taught it, while Pharisees taught the election of a few, and Sadducees denied, He said, "Blessed are the poor in spirit, for theirs is the kingdom of heaven." It was a new view, because, though perfectly well known in the earliest, childlike age, it had been lost sight of in the day of brutish degeneracy. When He went to the tomb of Lazarus He met with the old view, as Martha said: "I know that he will rise again in the resurrection at the last day;" and swiftly He controverted it with the truth, "Whosoever liveth and believeth in me shall never die." When Sadducees came to argue, with the dilemma which no Pharisee could have solved with his theology, the Lord let in the light at once, and said: "God is not the God of the dead, but of the living; ye therefore do greatly err." When the last trial came He taught by his very bearing a view which was the same He had been teaching all along. Phariseeism could not have said what He did. Sadduceeism could not have opened its mouth. But He said: "Let not your heart be troubled, I go to prepare a place for you." On the cross the repentant thief uttered the best faith he knew when he said, "Lord, remember me when thou comest into thy kingdom." In that far distant day he hoped to be remembered. The swift answer was, "To-day thou shalt be with me in paradise."

But more than all teaching was his own example. He awaited no last-day resurrection. After a brief period He was again with the disciples, though no longer needing the opening of a door that He might enter. Thus He had fulfilled the promise which had been forgotten, which is so widely forgotten now, "After two days will He revive us. In the third day He will raise us up, and we shall live in His sight."

This was the third view, and its history may be briefly told. It flourished for a time, though not fully understood. The Revelation made to John about sixty years after our Lord's resurrection, confirmed it. The belief in salvation, in a spiritual body, and in a spiritual world to be entered immediately after death, sustained the martyrs at the stake. But gradually there was falling away as to every doctrine of Christianity. The disputes at the Council of Nice about the Lord's nature and personality, show a great decline, or, rather, relapse on this point, and the other doctrines suffered likewise. At length the claim of control over men's future lives was asserted, and money was demanded for ransoming them from future punishment. And when this was asserted, the

Reformation arose and denied it; but this soon adopted the opinions of Calvin, who was educated as a lawyer and had been an excellent one, and who founded his system on the cold and severe precepts of Roman law. By this law a man's sin attainted with loss of caste all his descendants; so came the idea of all having sinned in Adam. All Calvin's earlier studies had taught him to regard the satisfaction of a debt as requiring the giving up of the person of the debtor to the will of the creditor, and in this way he pictured the life of our Lord as a satisfaction of the divine justice, wrought out by bodily sufferings and penalties.

Thus the third view was again lost, and men were divided between the two others, neither of which was true, when the Lord gave the truth again to the world, this time fully and finally. Having led a devout man along through studies and meditations, by which his mind became prepared to comprehend the laws of the spiritual world, He at length fulfilled the promise of His second coming by teaching this man, Swedenborg, out of the Holy Word the facts of the hereafter, and all the truth needed to be received among men ere the Lord could inaugurate the age of His second advent, or, more correctly, second and final presence.

On this particular point, the nature of the eternal life, this revelation gave the world a third view, the third view of to-day, as it was that of early Christianity. And as it was the true one then, the Lord's view as contrasted with that of men, the Scriptural view as distinguished from that of the Rabbis, so it is to-day. Its assertions are simply: There is another world; it is real; it is to this world what the soul is to the body; its nature is spiritual, as that of this world is natural; into it men enter at death by putting off their material bodies which they never resume; the life there is unending. As to good and evil, this view is, that those who have fully matured their characters here do not radically change them after death, that those who are evil are in a condition of restraint, and that those who are willing to abide by the order of divine law are most blessedly free and joyful, but that both classes are in the performance of uses. Moreover, all who die as infants and children, and all those of heathen religions who have conformed to their principles of right, become also of the heavenly company. The life of the angels is an unending progression in administering the uses of heaven, and the nature of their employment is known from the saying that they came and ministered to our Lord in his trials. Ministering — does not this express it? By all their various gifts, in the development of which the uses of this life gave them an apprenticeship, they minister to the Lord forever, serving Him without fear, in holiness and righteousness before Him all the days of their lives.

In regard to this view, it may be remarked at once that it is better than the others on several accounts:

I. It is of the Lord's spirit. We know Him in his works, and we know that He is not in them what He has sometimes been pictured. Sending his rain on the just and the unjust, making his sun to rise on the evil and on the good, He is not to be viewed as narrow, partial, vindictive, but as the All-Father. The absolute sovereignty of a Roman master is not the type of God, for we have seen Him revealed, and learned that He is merciful and gracious.

II. Moreover, as has been amply indicated, this view is scriptural, being the very one brought out in the teachings of our Lord.

III. It is also more worthy to be held by reasonable beings than the others. Ignorance, whether Sadducean or agnostic, though sometimes boasted of, is not worthy of rational beings. It is really a childish obstinacy, or perhaps a temporary despair, which cries out, "We know nothing, and can know nothing of the supernatural." A loftier courage and faith would be much more becoming. And, on the other hand, to hold that God is of such a sort that civilized laws cannot copy Him, is surely unworthy. Who punishes the child with the father to the degree of making him equally guilty? Who denies the heathen man all right to an equal chance? Not good laws, and, therefore, not God, even if some so allege for Him but really against Him.

IV. Tried by the test of affording motive to good life, the third is immeasurably the superior of the previous views. What motive has he who has no hope, or but a slender one? He may do what he can for those about him, and do it unselfishly, but must there not be despair in his own heart?

Take this despair from him, set his eye on a great future for all, bid him prepare himself every day and hour for an unending life in a real world where order and beauty reign, in a real body which knows neither death nor pain, in the presence of God, whom he will no longer dread save as he is ashamed of his own unworthiness to be beloved by one so holy; show him that this is from the Bible itself, is what the Lord taught, and has given anew to the world; bid him remember that his highest life is the most loving and wise cöoperation with that

Lord in his great and beneficent purposes; and will not his eye kindle, his heart rejoice, his hand grasp more firmly the implements of his toil? ."The angels came and ministered." Let him ponder upon it. Not unsubstantial ghosts were they, but radiant departed spirits; and ministering was their nobleness, their bliss. Let him come with all his heart to love that service, in sickness and in health, in good repute and evil repute; and when the time comes to go hence, let him say: "Lord Jesus, receive my spirit." "He shall enter in through the gates into the city," and be "as the angels of God in heaven."

MAN A SPIRIT.

"Immediately I was in the Spirit."—REV. iv. 2.

WHERE was he? What was the region in which he saw the Lord, the angels and the Holy City? Where are any, or where will they be, when, if ever, they are "in the spirit," and see the multitudes of the departed?

It may be that other questions are of more immediate importance, in that the answers of them bear more directly upon every-day duties; but no question could be more interesting. When one holds up a grain of sand and endeavors to compare it with the mountain, every cubic foot of which contains the grain a myriad times; or, when one catches a rain-drop upon the finger and seeks to compare it with the great deep, whose every wave is made of ten thousand such drops,— he still obtains no adequate comparison between the life that now is and that which is to come. The one exists for a day, a year, at most for a century; the other, beginning where this leaves off, goes on forever. Men take a few steps, and die, and an unending path is then entered upon.

Do not all need to know something of that other sphere, which will soon receive them, and at whose open door they may be already standing?

Sad indeed would they be if condemned to ignorance on this subject,— not only sad when those they love depart to this other state, but on their own accounts, since mystery is always unpleasant.

But John was there, and returned, and told his story; and the Lord' caused him to do so for the world's sake. Let all then, so far as they may properly do so, endeavor to accompany him, and to learn whither he went, and how.

Beginning by considering what all can easily understand, the first remark shall be that John appears to have made no bodily journey. He says he was *immediately* in the spirit, and that would imply no change of bodily location. Nor was this possible, for he was on an island to which he had been banished to prevent his preaching, and there he must remain.

No, he made no bodily journey. Nor shall others. When they come to die and to see the other world, their bodies will be quiet. The journeys by rail or sea will all have been taken, and if they are at the moment upon a journey, it need not be continued.

Furthermore, it is an idea easy to form that John, although he came to be present with the departed, was not required to go through such a change as has been supposed necessary. He did not even need to die, as is seen from the fact that he afterward wrote and spoke of all he saw. His body did not need to be buried and then await a judgment day, and come forth, and be put together again, and resume its place on this earth, which had by some means been freed from the evil and from all the effects of their wickedness. On the contrary, the change was made immediately, and if nothing else would do so, this single text would deal a fatal blow to the old ideas of long waiting in the grave and sudden reawakening to life.

The next point about which there is really no room for doubt is that the objects which he saw, and about which men are told in this Book of Revelation, were real objects, and not mere visions of the brain. It is clear that John saw and described the appearance of the Lord, and that he heard His words. If the Lord's world be real, so much more is He Himself; and, in coming before His face, John came into a reality in comparison with which the island of Patmos, where his body was, was but a shadow.

Moreover, he saw angels, and would have worshipped one of them, but the angel said, "See thou do it not, for I am thy fellow-servant, and of thy brethren the prophets and of them that keep the sayings of this book." (REV. xxii. 9.) He also saw a great multitude which was said to be of all nations and kindreds and tongues, and these were certainly the people or of the people who had departed this life.

He also saw a city of magnificent description, and was told that the nations of those who were saved would enter into it, and that the glory of the Lord lightened it. Thus the city was as real as the nations and as the Lord.

Much more of equal reality was seen and described with equal exactness, but these suffice to show that at once he came into a state in which he saw objects before invisible to him, and which would have continued to be invisible to him, but for the Divine permission and assistance.

Next, it is clearly apparent that John was, for the time at least, in the other world,— in the companionship and amid the scenes which he would have enjoyed if already removed from this life and established in the life hereafter.

The island of Patmos, desolate, lonely, a mere place of banishment, could not afford the views portrayed in this book of the Holy Word. Nor could any other part of this earth, or of the sky, have presented such scenes. He was not in Asia, but in the spirit, and must have been in some other sphere than the earthly in order to see and to hear what he saw and heard.

His bodily eyes, suited to receive impressions only from material things, could not behold the throne. His ears, capable of reporting only the vibrations of our air, could not have heard the anthems of the angelic choirs. Nor could his hand of flesh take up anything but what was of the substance of matter; it could not take the little book (Ch. x.) out of the hand of the mighty angel "whose face was as it were the sun, and his feet like pillars of fire."

Is there any real room for doubt that he was for the time in heaven, that he had powers which enabled him to be there, that he had these powers while still in the body, that they were not the powers of the body, these being inadequate to the purpose, that in order to come into the use of these powers he took no bodily journey, nor passed through the change of death, and that nevertheless his contact with the other life was real and full?

So far thought has been given to John and to his experience with an implied intention to conclude from him to others, and to learn of others' powers and possibilities as to coming into the spirit, when the Lord shall call them from this life.

Before doing so, however, and in order to do so, it will be of use to consider that it is made a matter of Scripture declaration that others have had similar experience. If this prove true, the matter becomes at once plain, and the conclusion is easy, that what John did was possible to all, and illustrates the general way in which men come into the other world, and tells where that other world is.

A striking case of similar admission, during this life and without a preparatory process of journey or essential change of any sort, is found in the sixth chapter of the second book of Kings. The prophet Elisha was pursued by a hostile band who surrounded his place of abode in the night. Next morning, his servant looked forth, and cried out, "Alas, my master, what shall we do?" And he answered, "Fear not, for they that be with us are more than they that be with them." And Elisha prayed, and said, "Lord, I pray thee, open his eyes, that he may see." "And the Lord opened the eyes of the young man; and he saw; and behold the mountain was full of horses and chariots of fire round about Elisha."

Thus the servant, though not different from other men, could be "immediately in the spirit," and could see what would have been invisible otherwise.

Such instances abound. Daniel came into the same state. He says (tenth chapter), "I lifted up mine eyes and looked," and he beheld a glorious figure. He adds, "I Daniel alone saw the vision; for the men that were with me saw not the vision; but a great quaking fell upon them so that they fled to hide themselves." This instance is striking, as showing that Daniel was admitted to a view which was not seen by others; and it declares that he and John and others required permission before they could enter this state.

.

But while these instances abound with the patriarchs and prophets of Old Testament time, they are none the less seen in the Gospel history.

At the time of the Lord's coming into the world, an angel, Gabriel, was seen by both Zacharias and Mary; and, while he had been unknown to them before, and was not seen again, for the time their admission to his presence was complete.

Angels, too, were seen by the shepherds, at Bethlehem, who also heard their chorus of joy over the Nativity.

Angels were seen by the women who came to the sepulchre, and were heard to say, "He is not here, he is risen."

And a remarkable example of this sort took place with the disciples, Peter, James and John, who went up into a mountain with their master, and no longer saw Him with their bodily eyes, in the face and garments which were commonly before them; but beheld him in glory, and Moses and Elias with Him; and these were then not in the flesh, and thus the Lord was seen with eyes like those by which He was seen by the angels, who ministered unto Him.

Thus John's case is seen to be but one of many, and to illustrate a general fact. Let this fact now be stated. Men have already the natures which belong to the other world. They have the faculties of sight, hearing, and so forth, which are required to make them alive in that world. But these are, for the time, clothed by a material body, and thus limited to the material world. Yet the man may be separated temporarily or permanently from the body, and then be cognizant of the events of the spiritual world. Thus, dying is simply doing permanently what John did for a short time, and what Elisha's servant, and Daniel, and Mary, did for short times, permission being granted for important purposes.

To the question where is the other world? where was John when in the spirit? the answer is now ready. He was not anywhere in this world. He left his body where it was; but he became conscious of a world not in this one, nor of it, but in which he could be present immediately.

Where is heaven? It is where men's spirits now are, though clothed and concerned with material bodies. It is where the departed are, because their covering of flesh has been removed. It is where others will consciously be when removed at death from their bodies. Now they are not conscious of that world, but their consciousness and all dependent faculties are engaged in this world. Sometime they shall be released from this world, and then no long journey nor delay will be required ere they enter upon the other, the spiritual, world.

It is possible, with the help of the unwise from the other side, to rend the veil and to become what are called spiritual mediums; but New-Churchmen realize more fully than all others that this is to infringe Divine Order, and to expose the soul to great dangers. It is the Lord's work to take men hence. It is theirs to wait for Him to do so. He in His Scripture is the guide of all men,— nor can any other be looked to as a safe Shepherd of the sheep.

To all this, which seems to be a clear and reasonable view, there is only one objection. It exalts one's idea of the Lord's mercy. It illumines the pages of Scripture with heavenly radiance. It bears most solemnly upon the present life; teaching with tremendous emphasis the need of preparation to depart, at any time and at once, to the world where the final home will be taken. It is most helpful in times of trial. It stretches forth before one at all times a vista of indescribable beauty.

But there is one objection, sufficient with the many, and that is that the idea is new. It seems incredible that Christian people should be disinclined to find new truth in the Scripture, but many have such a feeling to their loss.

What is new truth? An invention, in the sense of a human production? Not at all. What was the discovery of the use of steam? It was simply the fact becoming known that a power had lain unused and unknown up to that time, but now had been revealed. So of the telegraph, so of the knowledge of astronomy, so of everything true. Once it was not known, but the fact was always there. At length, under Divine Providence, it was seen.

Then came glad reception by some, but prejudices had always to be conquered. The Church itself forced Galileo to conceal his new knowledge of the fact that the earth revolved about the sun, and the Church in that day of its extreme ignorance held the idea concerning the other world which the majority of its members hold to-day.

But what was plain to Galileo has now become plain to all, and thus what was plain to Swedenborg is slowly becoming plain to all. They see that a glorious truth, contained all the time in Scripture, was not made known at first.

Object because an idea is new! Why not object to the discovery of the power of electricity because it was not discovered a thousand years earlier? It was discovered when the Lord saw the fit time had come. So also of this new view of death, and blessed be He who allows it to be made known in our day. "The people that walked in darkness have seen a great light: they that dwell in the land of the shadow of death, upon them hath the light shined."

The application of this truth needs but few words.

The other world is always near. It is no distant part of our planet. It is not to be reached by any long journey. There is to be no delay in the oblivion of the grave. Thus there will be no time for preparation after leaving this life, before entering upon the other. As men live, they die; as they die, they live again, the same in nature, whether in some degree of purification from evil, or with every harmful habit in full strength.

Nor have they necessarily any long warning. John had none on that Lord's day. The disciples had none when they went up into the mountain. Others may have none, but some day, as they go about their daily tasks, may depart from the flesh forever.

That all will go at some time or other is certain, and that this life is a preparation for the other is declared everywhere in Scripture. "Behold," saith the Lord, "I come quickly, and my reward is with me to give every man according as his work shall be."

Are all ready, or are they trying to become so? Are their affairs so ordered that, if they go hence to-morrow, no accusation of unfaithfulness will blot their memory? Are they trying to learn to work, and to work in the heavenly way, so that, when they come into the spirit, there may be neither reluctance at the new duty nor undue laboriousness in its performance? Are they at peace with all? Are they trying to act with the Lord, not burying the talent beneath a corroding earth of selfish indulgence, but seeking to increase it for His sake? Are they as those who "wait for their lord when he will return from the wedding, that when he cometh and knocketh, they may open to him immediately?"

Finally, let all remember,—in sickness and health, when they see friends removed from the flesh, and when new souls enter this world,—let them remember that, as John was "immediately in the spirit," and as others are spoken of in Scripture as having had similar experience, they may conclude that the great other world already possesses them as to the spiritual part, but that for the time they are clothed in flesh, and their consciousness limited to this world; and that the process of death is but the change of consciousness; and that no lingering in graves, till the earth shall rend, is revealed as God's truth.

> " But they shall walk in robes of white,
> With kings and priests abroad;
> And they shall summer high in bliss,
> Upon the hills of God."

DEATH.

"Not dead, but sleepeth."—LUKE viii. 52.

THE question, "Is there a life hereafter?" has given place, in the advancement of the age, to the question, "Of what nature is the life hereafter?" And, while this is engrossing the attention of many, a few have progressed to some clearness of comprehension on this latter point, and are now interested in a third question, namely, "How do we come from this life into the other?" "By what process," they would ask, "with what sensations, if with any, are we removed from the material body, and introduced to scenes now invisible?"

When one is attempting to form some notion of a new thing, he is wont to ask first, "What is it like?" If the answer implies that it is something not in the least resembling any object of previous knowledge, the expectation of coming to any adequate understanding of the new object is instantly checked. If, however, he can learn that it resembles, even in the least degree, a matter of previous acquaintance, he can learn the difference in form or other qualities; and, without having seen it or being sure that he is right, he has some rest in his notion.

Thus, if to one in the full enjoyment of this life, and quite unacquainted with the phenomenon of death, a friend should say, "Death will come to you sooner or later," a responsive interest would lead him to ask a description of death. "It is a change," might be returned. "Of what sort?" would be the next question; and here there would be hesitation, and at last an answer varying to suit the informant's religious views.

Suppose the question to be put by one thoroughly in earnest. It may be pressed by the child who listens with dread to the labored breathing of its sick parent, and longs to know what is to come; or, brought to look upon the silent face which it shall never see again, stands tearful and hushed, and wonders what is this? It may be the question of the grown man who marches to the battle, side by side with his tried comrade, and in an hour sees that comrade lie, unheeding the tumult, and giving no answer to the shout of victory. It may be the gentle seeking of the aged, whose hands are no longer strong in holding the implements of toil, and who patiently await the final hour, yet knowing not what it will bring.

With all these the question is one, a beseeching cry for light, though it be but a ray; a prayer for an answer, though it be but a word. "What is death?" they ask. "What takes place *in articulo mortis*, in that momentous instant of time in which the hold upon this world, which may have lasted nearly a century, is irrevocably relaxed?"

Attending first to the view which has most often been taken, it may be stated that that theory of the resurrection which implies that the other life is in the far distant future, to be inaugurated at the judgment-day, and to be enjoyed only by the elect, who are to be restored to this earth, which is itself at the same time to be purified by fire, is a view which gives at once the most decided and most unwelcome answer to the question. This view as once held by all Christian people, and as held by not a few at the present day, should first be considered. It will be found to give, as has been said, a plain answer. "Is death like anything with which I am acquainted?" The answer as so rendered is simply, No, an irreversible and appalling No!

To suppose that a man can have any acquaintance with a state of being in which his life is in any sense suspended for centuries is an absurdity. He knows about various forms of life and states of existence, but coming to an end, or coming so near to an end that he cannot be said to live in a body, is to him the very blackness of darkness, the utter absence of a notion. Yet, from this point of view, no other answer can be had. The words may be varied. Death may be described as that process by which existence is suspended, or as the undoing of the tie which binds to life; but the light breaks not in to drive away the chill which the very word brings with it. " Wait, and God will show you what it is; be patient and not fearful:" this may be answered, and nothing more.

The idea that the resurrected dead are to occupy this earth is indissolubly connected with the idea that the divine mercy in prolonging life is to be limited to a small portion of the human race. It matters not that by the adoption of a date for the commencement of human life upon this earth, which indeed would be credited only by the ignorant, it may be made conceivably possible for some part of those who have died to return, and to find standing-room. The thought of God's annihilating any part of His human creatures is too repulsive to survive, and it loses ground every day. And, in its company, departs also that notion of death which implies a long waiting, in the grave or elsewhere, for restoration to life.

If this idea be departing, it will be right to turn from its answer in search of another, and to put the same inquiry to that steadily increasing company gathered from all parts of the Christian Church and from without it, and consisting of those who believe that the other world even now is, and that it is inhabited by those who have departed this life in all time since the Creator introduced man into existence. They believe this other world to be one of spiritual substance, and therefore not visible to the outward and material eye, but which is perfectly real, and which has at certain times been rendered cognizable to men and women of whom we read, especially in the Scriptures, and thus that the glorious visions of the prophets were glimpses of the wonders of this heavenly world.

To those who take this inspiring view of the hereafter, the question which now engages attention still remains, though it loses something of its absorbing interest. For there are those so child-like in faith that, when once convinced of the truth of the future existence, they easily await the process by which they are to obtain it, be that process painful or agreeable, of longer or shorter duration.

But, apart from these, there will still remain many who are more than ever ready to investigate the change called death, because they are more than ever hopeful of obtaining an understanding of the matter.

Speaking for those who believe in a real life hereafter, into which men are ushered upon finishing the earthly existence, the partial reply may be made that death is not a long journey through space; for all idea of the spiritual world as distant in space must be excluded as gross and sensuous.

It may also be suggested that death is probably not an instantaneous or forcible projecting of the individual into another sphere of existence. It would be impossible to show any reason why this should be so, and why this alone of all processes, either of growth or decay, should not be gradual. Certainly, no one who looks upon the face of a deceased person, often becoming full of a new beauty and seeming to smile, will be inclined to believe that there has been any sudden blazing upon the sight of a strong and unaccustomed light.

The teaching of the Scripture supports the argument here. That frame, through which had flowed the blessed influences which gave sight to the blind and hearing to the deaf, was crucified, was buried, and rose again. Having arisen, it was not known by those who had been the daily companions of the Saviour, nor was shut out by doors, but entered to the secreted disciples. The conclusion is that it was such a body as was adapted to the other world, and that the process of death had been performed. While no one doubts this, let it be remembered that this process occupied some part of three days, and that this single case would lead men to believe that death is not a sudden, but a gradual surrender of the earthly powers. As if to leave no doubt upon the subject, it is expressly declared in HOSEA vi., apparently as of universal application, that "after two days will He revive us: in the third day He will raise us up, and we shall live in His sight."

The conclusion is thus arrived at, that a much clearer view of death results from the new than from the old view of the hereafter, and that the weight of reasoning and the direct statements of Scripture, favor the idea that death is so gradual a cessation of bodily life as to continue till the third day.

This is vastly better than total ignorance upon the subject, but it is evidently only an approximation to an answer to the oft-repeated question. It may be however, that still more light can be had, and for this purpose the pages of the Bible are confidently turned.

It has been said that many entertain the belief that the prophets, in some instances, were admitted while still in the flesh to the realities of the other life. This idea is not only reasonable in itself, but it is also an extremely comforting thought as leading one to believe that God intends in this way to make men beforehand acquainted with that which is to come. It is also frequently and directly stated in these visions, that the inspired person saw and conversed with angels, or with the spirits of the departed. It will occur to mind instantly, that to obtain an idea of the process by which these prophets were introduced into the spiritual world is to take a long step toward understanding the phenomenon of death. One cannot attempt to follow this process in the case of different persons without perceiving that, in many instances, the individual was led into the sphere of the hereafter through sleep. And the whole labor, on their part, was simply to fall asleep.

Daniel saw at one time (Ch. viii.) a combat between a ram and a he-goat, and heard one saint speaking, and another saint answering. Soon the angel Gabriel came to instruct him in the meaning of the vision. It must appear that, at this time, he was veritably present in the spiritual world. How had he obtained entrance thither? "Now, as he was speaking unto me, I was in a deep sleep on my face, toward the ground; but he touched me, and set me upright." He had fallen asleep, and the angel spoke to him, awaking him to knowledge of spiritual things.

Again (Ch. x.) Daniel saw a personage whose appearance was of the same glorious nature with that described by other prophets, and by John in the Revelation, as one "like unto the Son of man." The way in which he came to see this being is thus described: "when I heard the voice of his words, then was I in a deep sleep on' my face; . . . and, behold, an hand touched me."

There is one passage to which one may constantly refer, while endeavoring to gain light upon this subject, because its statements are exceedingly clear. The account of the Lord's transfiguration brings indisputably to view the fact that, hundreds of years after their decease, two persons were made visible to men. Moses and Elias were seen to talk with the Lord. They had died, and were now in the spiritual world; consequently, in seeing them, the three disciples, Peter, James, and John, were admitted temporarily to a participation in the scenes of the other life. The question is, in what way was this done? "But Peter and they that were with him, were heavy with sleep; and when they were awake, they saw His glory, and the two men that stood with Him."

In this case, as in the two preceding, we are informed of the sleep, after some part of the vision is described, as if they fell asleep and seemed to themselves to dream what they saw, and were at length awaked, but with no interruption of the vision. They slept, and dreamed into full wakefulness in the angelic company.

Other instances of sleep, as a means of bringing persons into a state of conscious communication with the heavenly world, might easily be adduced. Thus in Genesis, Ch. xv. it is said that "a deep sleep fell upon Abram," upon which the future of his race was revealed to him. Job says, (Ch. xxxiii.) "In a dream, in a vision of the night, when deep sleep falleth upon man, in slumberings upon the bed, then He openeth the ears of men." And this he said, out of his own experience (Ch. iv.): "In thoughts from the visions of the night, when deep sleep falleth upon men, . . . then a spirit passed before my face. . . . It stood still, but I could not discern the form thereof. An image was before mine eyes; there was silence and I heard a voice, saying, 'Shall mortal man be more just than God? Shall a man be more pure than his Maker?'" It is written by Zechariah the prophet (Ch. iv.) "And the angel that talked with me, came again and waked me, as a man is wakened out of his sleep; and said unto me, What seest thou?" Of Elijah, also, it is said (1 KINGS, Ch. xix.) "And as he lay and slept under a juniper-tree, behold, then an angel touched him."

An apparent rejoinder to this argument would be to say that the sleep of the prophets and disciples undoubtedly resulted from natural causes, as from weariness, and was not induced for the purpose suggested. But this does not in the least invalidate the inference. The statement is not as to the cause of their sleep; but their sleep being from whatever cause, it is argued that this was then accompanied with a wakening of the inward sight to spiritual scenes.

Every one knows how varied are the causes of death; but the question is concerning the process of death, which is presumably the same in all cases, since the event is always a transfer of the consciousness from this world to the next.

Certain instances may therefore be adduced in Bible history, showing that a virtual transfer of the mind to the future world and to the presence of the departed has been made by sleep. By many this will be regarded as sufficient. They will remember that sleep is frequently spoken of in the Scriptures as the equivalent of death; and though, in the Old Testament, this sleep is described as gloomy and lasting, in the New it is made plain that it is but the gentle way of passing the door which openeth to immortality.

When the martyr Stephen stood before his accusers, "and all that sat in the council, looking upon him, saw his face as it had been the face of an angel," he boldly and sweetly laid before them his faith; but "they cried out with a loud voice, and stopped their ears, and ran upon him with one accord, and cast him out of the city and stoned him. And he kneeled down and cried with a loud voice, 'Lord, lay not this sin to their charge.' And when he had said this, he fell asleep." He heard no longer the jeers of the multitude, nor felt the sharp pain as their missiles bruised his flesh: he had fallen asleep, and his Lord would wake him to the presence of those who like him had borne, and had been patient; and death would be for ever passed.

The Lord said of the daughter of the ruler, "she is not dead, but sleepeth;" telling that what they supposed to be virtual extinction was not such, but only a yielding of the mind and body to sleep, whence at His word she would awake. He said, to be sure, at another time, "Lazarus is dead;" but this was for the reason that the disciples misconstrued His first words, "Our friend Lazarus sleepeth."

The question, which has been considered, is one

for which many would seek a scientific answer, relying more upon the observation of physicians than upon revelation. But all should rely upon both, letting the one assist the other. The following, taken from the "Popular Science Review," are the words of an eminent English surgeon upon this very point. He says, "At his entrance into the world, man sleeps into existence and awakens into knowledge. At his exit from the world, he dozes into sleep, and sleeps into death." And he continues in a passage of remarkable beauty, in a description of the perfectly natural death, as several times observed by him in all its stages: "The faculties of the mind which have been intellectual, without pain, or anger, or sorrow, lose their way, retire, rest. Ideas of time and place are gradually lost; ambition ceases; repose is the one thing asked for, and sleep day by day gently and genially whiles away the hours. The wakings are short, painless, careless, happy; awakenings to a busy world, to hear sounds of children at play, to hear just audibly gentle voices offering aid and comfort, and to talk a little on simple things. At last, without pain or struggle or knowledge of the coming event, the deep sleep that falls so often is the sleep perpetual, euthanasia."

These are the words of one whose object it is to speak only of the physical death. He paints but the outline of the picture; he describes but the first stage of the happy journey. Softly again will the mind awake, and without surprise or fear, for the awakening is to the presence of those departed already, towards whom the soul has yearned for long years; to the presence of the lamented parent or consort or child, to a holy reunion, to a sacred and restful welcome home. As the weary bark glides from the heaving sea into the smooth harbor; so, softly and dreamily, the weary one removes from the material body, from sorrow and death and crying, to the green pastures and still waters of the life beyond.

It matters not how violent has been the illness, how agonized the frame. As, when the man is suddenly struck down, he can afterwards remember nothing but a shock and the reawakening among his friends, while all the tumult of the disaster is a perpetual blank; so, looking back in the hereafter, men will remember only that they fell asleep in one world, and waked in another, fell asleep as they do every night and waked as they do every morning, except that the scene soon became changed, and was inexpressibly more lovely.

This, then, should be one's confidence in health, and this the glorious prospect of the hereafter; while, for the change, let it not be feared; but rather let all look forward gladly to coming to the end of this life, and into the company of the beloved departed.

> " Sustained and soothed
> By an unfaltering trust, approach thy grave,
> Like one that wraps the drapery of his couch
> About him, and lies down to pleasant dreams. "

THE LORD'S EXAMPLE IN DEATH.

"He will swallow up death in victory."— ISAIAH xxv. 8.

WHEN our Lord came among men, He found them regarding death with superstitious dread. They held somewhat different views in respect to it; but all their views were false and fearful. Some believed that till the last day they would lie in their graves, and that the righteous among them would then rise from the earth, while the rest would not awake. Some thought that the resurrection would extend only to the Jews; others thought that only the graves about Jerusalem and those into which some earth from Jerusalem had been cast, would be opened. Some could find no ground for this, or any faith on this point, in the law or prophets, and refused to accept the teaching of the Rabbis.

The best view held at that day was expressed

by Martha, at the grave of Lazarus, when she said, "I know that he will rise again in the resurrection at the last day." At some remote period, a catastrophe would rend the earth, and the righteous brother would come forth, after his long sleep, to dwell again by the holy city. This was all. There was no knowledge of spiritual life, of life apart from flesh, of a kingdom not of this world. Death had fallen like a blight upon the family, taking away its head, to the earthy dungeon, and, when funeral rites, which were mere wailing, had been performed, there was no more to be done except to go daily to the grave, and lament the irrecoverable loss. Their only consolation, if such it could be called, was expressed in the Word, thus: "Call for the mourning women that they may come; let them make haste and take up a wailing for us. . . . Let mine eyes run down with tears night and day, and let them not cease." (JER. ix. 17; xiv. 17.)

He came to these, sitting thus in the "shadow of death," and by His words, and especially by His example, did "guide their feet into the way of peace." It is evident that, to people so devoid of spiritual thought, no clear idea of the other world could be presented. "If I have told you earthly things and ye believe not, how shall ye believe if I tell you of heavenly things?" But if He might not speak to them all the truth, He could give them an example.

That He early became aware of the presence of the angels, and of their helpful companionship, we can see from many of His words, as when He spake of the angels guarding little children, and of those who took the poor beggar to be with Abraham. The fact of His birth without human paternity led Him early to His true Father, and with that Father in heaven He learned to commune. This brought the angels to Him, and, as with those of the Golden Age, they were manifestly present, ministering in times of temptation, and speaking with Him on mountains, in night watches, of the death He should accomplish at Jerusalem.

Two facts He could show the people, and they,

if they acknowledged them, would be lifted up above their dread, and be enabled to meet death calmly, thenceforth, and till a time of fuller revelation should come. First, He could show them that He understood it, and did not dread it; secondly, that He was lord over it, and could deliver from it, that is, from all the terrors which had attended it.

So He foretold His own death peacefully, saying, "I go unto the Father." "I lay down my life that I may take it again." "I go to prepare a place for you." So He stopped the funeral procession coming out of Nain, and gave the son back to his mother. So He went in where the hired mourners were lamenting over Jairus's daughter, and took her by the hand, and said, "Little maid, arise;" and she was alive again. So He went up to Bethany, after one had been dead four days, and, while He mingled His own tears with those of His heart-broken friends, He bade them roll away the stone and called to Lazarus within, and gave him to his people again,—a living witness of the fact that He was "the resurrection and the life."

To the Sadducees, whose contempt for mere traditions led them to deny the common belief, He showed that in the law itself there was teaching as to the eternal life. To His disciples, on the last night, He spoke of His going away, and when they questioned Him further, showing that they knew nothing as yet of the heavens, He answered, "I am the Way, the Truth, and the Life." "Let not your heart be troubled; neither let it be afraid."

He must himself die, because thus He would fulfil all the law of human life, thus giving up the infirmities He had borne in order that He might encounter and overcome all the enemies of man. And He would have died very gently, perhaps falling asleep during some twilight prayer, but that the hatred of man which had hitherto pursued Him, demanded leave to regard Him as a felon, and to seek by torture to destroy Him, and to stamp out all the brotherliness He had inculcated.

Thus had they been permitted to abuse the Holy Word and its prophets, though they could not destroy. Thus would the unutterable mercy of the Lord permit them to order the death He should die, seeing that its great triumph they could not lessen. He had said, "Unto him that smiteth thee on the one cheek, offer also the other," and He said this because He loved submissiveness rather than vengeance.

He bore without resistance the unjust inquisition of Annas and Caiaphas. He stood still, bound and already exhausted, while the council heard its false witnesses, and uttered its decision against Him. He went quietly to stand before Pilate, and then to Herod, and then to Pilate again. The face was already bruised and bleeding from the abuse of the soldiers; but He bowed without complaint and bore the dreadful scourging until they dared to torture Him no longer, lest failing strength should rob them of the satisfaction of inflicting upon Him that most frightful of deaths, unknown to Jews, unworthy of the vilest Romans, inflicted only upon slaves,— the death by crucifixion.

It was near ten o'clock in the forenoon, in a season as heated as our midsummer, when a guard of Roman soldiers led through the streets of Jerusalem three prisoners, each bleeding from many wounds, each tottering under the weight of two bars bound upon the arms and crossed upon the back of the neck,— and one of these was He who had been teaching men how to die. Verily, the teaching was come to the proof.

A crowd lined the way, and joined the procession as it passed. How could the women fail to weep when they saw Him sinking beneath His load, "His visage was so marred, more than any man, and His form more than the sons of men?" But He said only, "Weep not for me, but for yourselves and your children." The future, which He knew, would bring them agonies which even now more moved Him than His wounds.

They reached the place; the soldiers kept back the crowd, while others executed the final deed.

At such times, horrid imprecations were wont to rend the air, while the nails were driven through the flesh. All that was heard from Him was, "Father, forgive them, they know not what they do." A touch of pity offered Him wine, mingled with myrrh, that it might stupefy the sufferer, and, in a degree, diminish the agony. "And when He had tasted, He would not drink." There was work for Him in that dread hour, lest the forces of hell, thronging upon Him, might, for an instant, prevail, and extort one thought of bitterness. Therefore "He would not drink."

The crowd scoffed Him with loud jeers. The two on either hand reviled Him. But the hours of the torrid noon passed and He made no answer, "even as the sheep before her shearers is dumb." The sun blistered the naked, festering flesh, but the spirit was looking above the flesh and the crowd. "The sorrows of death compassed me, and the pains of hell got hold upon me. I found distress and sorrow. Then called I upon the name of the Lord; O Lord, I beseech thee, deliver my soul."

The voice of another was heard at length above the taunts. It was one of the thieves who spoke. Overcome by the very presence and bearing of Him whom he first reviled, he prayed, "Lord, remember me when thou comest into thy kingdom." And in tones as sweet as when He spake the Beatitudes, He answered, "To-day thou shalt be with me in paradise."

Anon, He saw in the crowd the figure of a woman, reckoned old in Palestine, a widow and disconsolate. It was the cousin of Elizabeth, the wife of the Nazarene carpenter; it was she whose piety was His first teacher. Utterly crushed now with her grief, as if a sword pierced her very soul, she stood with the beloved disciple, and looked upon her dying Lord, once her first-born babe. Again He spake in tones of infinite pity, "Woman, behold thy son;" and to the dear disciple, "Behold thy mother." Command of sweet gratitude for all she had done and suffered; fair reward,— to be taken home and tenderly cared for by the gentlest of the disciples till she should enter into her rest!

It was now three o'clock. Six hours of agony had passed. The end was near. Laying aside the Greek speech, which was used in conversing with the rulers and others at Jerusalem, He uttered, in the tongue of Nazareth, the words of the twenty-second Psalm, beginning, "*Eloi, eloi, lama sabacthani.*" The Psalm applied to that day, for it continues, "All they that see me laugh me to scorn. My tongue cleaveth to my jaws. They pierced my hands and my feet. I may tell all my bones; they look and stare upon me."

"I thirst," He said at length. A soldier dipped a sponge upon a reed in sour wine, and touched His lips in order to prolong the martyrdom. A momentary strength returned. The end had come. "It is finished," He said. "Father, into thy hands I commend my spirit." And saying these words, with a great voice, which hushed the crowd to silence, He, "the Resurrection and the Life," "swallowed up death in victory," and "the stone which the builders refused became the head-stone of the corner."

On the third day, freed from all fleshly infirmity, He showed himself to His disciples; and several other times during the forty days following, He supplemented the example of His death with the evident fact of continued and enlarged life, thereby taking from them all fear of death by giving them an all-controlling trust in Him. "Whether we live," said Paul, "we live unto the Lord, and whether we die, we die unto the Lord; whether therefore we live or die, we are the Lord's" (ROM. xiv. 8). And the accounts of the martyrs are full of evidence to the effect that from the Christian the dread of death was utterly removed.

In the present age, we may read the story of our Lord's life on earth in a new light. We may look from a spiritual point of view upon a work which has hitherto been viewed only on the natural side, and we may therefore enter more deeply into the meaning of His words and acts. This the best scholars of the day are assisting us to do by their wonderful thoroughness of research into all the story. So contemplating it, we should be the more deeply moved by it. After His example we should live, and in our dying we also should seek to be patient, peaceful, prayerful, in order that the sting of death, which is sin, may have no power, and that, coming into His higher world, we may "enter into the joy of our Lord." In the light of His example,—

> " There is no death! what seems so is transition;
> This life of mortal breath
> Is but a suburb of the life elysian,
> Whose portal we call Death."

RESURRECTION.

"And many of them that sleep in the dust of the earth shall awake, some to everlasting life, and some to shame and everlasting contempt."— DANIEL xii. 2.

THE idea that men die to live again at once is now quite generally received. In ancient times it was very well known, as is learned from the Egyptian records and other remains of antiquity, that to die was to enter upon another life, in which there would be, for those who were able to receive it, a most peaceful existence.

At a later day this bright conviction was somewhat obscured, and men failed to distinguish between the body laid in the grave and the spirit which had departed from it. They thought the natural body was the man, and that he was gone down to the under-world, and as this did not comport with their idea of the reward of righteousness, they believed the body would be raised again, and given to the spirit.

This led to burying bodies in the place where the spirits would desire to be, namely, close to the city Jerusalem, and it led to loud and long continued mourning at the grave, without any thought about another life in which the friend was at rest.

The Lord's teaching sought to dispel this gloomy ignorance. In His Sermon on the Mount He spoke of the meek, the pure, and the merciful as blessed, and so broke down at once the class-distinction which had given the possibility of resurrection only to the Pharisees. And then He went farther and said that, instead of a resurrection at the last day, those who lived and believed in Him should never die. At the last especially He bade the disciples believe that they would soon go to be with Him where He was and where He would prepare a place for them. And to the thief, who asked to be remembered when He should come into His kingdom, He said that that very day they would be together in paradise.

This light continued to shine among the early Christians. They did not think of the grave, but of going to dwell with Him. The inscriptions upon the Catacombs, as well as the words of the Apostolic writers, are full of this hope. "She follows a larger life, she has joy in the mansion of Christ," may still be seen where it was written of the Christian maiden, Theodora, fifteen hundred years ago.

There was a lapse of faith in this respect, a return to the Jewish idea from the Christian, and tombstones now standing reveal the fact that the early Christian conviction did not last. But now again, and with no likelihood of another return of darkness, the light is shining. "He is not here, but is risen," can again be said at the tomb, and, with more and more general acceptance, the idea prevails that the last day of the Scripture promises is not a day of bodily resurrection, but a day, a season, of revival of Christian religiousness.

Yet there remain, and will remain, in the Scriptures certain passages which apparently teach precisely the doctrine of the Pharisees, and which seem to stand opposed alike to the ancient idea, to our Lord's teaching and the faith of His followers, and to the convictions of many to-day. What shall be done with such a passage as this?—"And many of them which sleep in the dust of the earth shall awake, some to everlasting life, and some to shame and everlasting contempt."

It is said in Ezekiel, that the prophet saw a valley full of bones, and saw them all re-uniting into bodies, as if to show how it would be at the last day; and the Lord said, "I will open your graves, and cause you to come up out of your graves, and bring you into the land of Israel." (EZEKIEL xxxvii. 12.)

And even in the Gospel of Matthew (xxvii. 2) it is said that, at the time of the crucifixion, "many bodies of saints which slept, arose, and came out of the graves after His resurrection, and went into the holy city, and appeared unto many."

Such passages are not to be explained away. It is not a wise treatment of the Holy Word which says, "It made a mistake, or it means nothing now." Whatever be the explanation, it must be such as not to interfere in the least with the reverence felt for the Word, and with the power it should have over men's lives. But if the light can be thrown through this and its companion passages, so that what is now obscure may become transparent, the Word will be still unharmed, and what was a cloud in the sky will become a window of heaven.

Only one principle needs to be applied to this and to all such passages. It needs interpretation. They who hold it firmly as to come literally true, and who hold other prophecy so, are in precisely the attitude of the Jews who insisted that our Lord was not fulfilling prophecy, and slew Him as an imposter. Yet He was prophecy in its very life, and after His resurrection He showed to the disciples how perfectly all had been fulfilled.

It was the misfortune of later Christianity that it went back to the Jewish manner of viewing prophecy in its letter, and so not in its spirit; for thus men looked, and still look, for just such an appearing of the Lord in glory as the Jews looked for to their bitter disappointment; and the idea that He comes by opening His Word and reforming His Church, and dwelling in the hearts of His children, therefore seems fanciful and even blameworthy. All the time, however, His own example and teachings have given to the world the law that the language of prophecy must be fulfilled in its spirit first, and in its letter only when such a fulfilment does not interfere with the higher one.

Another idea now follows in course. The literal fulfilment of a prophecy may, in the nature of the other world, take place there when it could not take place here. Here the Lord was a lamb only in spirit, there He was seen by John as the Lamb. Here He was in outward reality but a Galilean, there He rode upon a white horse, and had upon His vesture and upon His thigh a name written, King of kings and Lord of lords. Here the promise that all kings should fall down before Him, and all nations serve Him, had no literal fulfilment, but there "a great multitude which no man could number, of all nations, and kindreds, and people, and tongues, stood before the throne and before the Lamb."

The miraculous of this world is the commonplace of heaven.

Not to follow this grand truth further, all can see that they should look to see such prophecies come true in spirit and letter in the other world, and in this world less fully as to the letter.

What then is the right way in which to read such prophecies? What is sleeping in the dust? Who are they that did so, and that rose after our Lord's resurrection, and who are they of Ezekiel's vision?

In the other life the angels dwell on high, the evil spirits below, and between them lies an intermediate place with which men on earth are directly associated and into which they first come after death. In support of this statement the whole language of the Scriptures may be cited. They always place heaven above, they always place hell beneath, and thus put men in an intermediate position. The account of the rich man lifting up his eyes to Abraham afar off, gives a vivid glimpse of the relations of spiritual position, which follow the laws of mental arrangement and spiritual attitude.

To the angels the earth and the men lately departed from it and still in close association with it, are as it were below, that is, below the expanses in which they are. The "souls under the altar," of the Book of Revelation, they that "sleep in the dust of the earth" of Daniel, "the saints which slept" of the Gospel, "the spirits in prison" of Peter's first Epistle and others similarly described are, in the light of heaven, not any persons imprisoned in our cemeteries, but such as were below the angels, in the lower parts of the intermediate sphere awaiting deliverance.

Were there such persons? Did the Lord, as one object of His coming, have in view the deliverance of such persons? When delivered, did they receive their final award?

Such judgment was indeed one of the Lord's purposes in His coming. The captivity into which the Israelites had fallen was political, but it was only the result, as every one knows, of their yielding themselves into a spiritual captivity, into a servitude wherein evil spirits, acting through evil passions, were the masters. The Old Testament is full of this, and of promises of deliverance. The Jews so expected it, but politically; the angels so expected it, but spiritually. They expected that those who lay below them in restraint would be delivered, and they were not mistaken, though the Jews' earthly expectations were doomed to disappointment. They so understood the passages which form the prophecies already cited, and, after the Lord's resurrection in triumph, they saw with joy the saints rising into their sphere, relieved of oppression by Him who came "to proclaim liberty to the captives."

Under Christianity, as under Judaism, the progress of events led to a captivity of which the Book of Revelation treats, and so mention is made of the "souls under the altar" who cried out, "How long will thou not judge and avenge our blood;" and they were bidden to rest for a time. Who the captors were in this case, who can doubt? A vast system of priestly domination, based upon the ignorance of the laity and enforced by torture of the rebellious, spread the whole width of Latin Christendom, claiming absolute power both here and over the keys of heaven. Men lived in servitude, died in it, rose in it, and remained in it till the Lord delivered them.

Of the mode of effecting the Last Judgment, which the interpretation of this Book shows to have already occurred, as indeed history fully indicates, this is not the place to treat, but let all note one passage from a later part of the Book which tells of what befell the imprisoned when deliverance came. "I looked, and lo, a Lamb stood on mount Zion, and with him an hundred forty and four thousand, having his Father's name written on their foreheads. And they sung as it were a new song. These were redeemed from among men, the first fruits unto God and the Lamb. Here is the patience of the saints, here are they that keep the commandments of God and the faith of Jesus."

On the other hand, Babylon, their haughty ruler, tottered and fell, and "shall be found no more at all."

Thus was the prophecy fulfilled; in its spirit and letter on high, in its spirit on earth. The vast multitude who had departed this life, and whose final award was hindered by the prevalence of priestcraft and mental servitude, and delayed till the Lord came to restore order, was separated into its true parts, and went its way to eternal habitations. Only the Lord could work such a judgment, and He performed it at the time when it was most necessary, and when its effects would be most permanent.

If only at His first coming men could have understood it thus, if they could have fully coöperated with Him, following Him gladly, how different the result might have been! As it was, He foresaw that He would have yet another judgment to perform, that again there would be sorrows, that His saints would be hated, that iniquity would abound, that the abomination would again stand in the holy place; "but," said He, "he that shall endure to the end, the same shall be saved."

In such a multitude as He delivered, not all would be ready to enter heaven. Some would place themselves on the right, and some on the left. There is a vital difference between an obedience that is sincere and one that is deceitful. The outward appearance may be the same, but He who "looketh on the heart" will see that one man loves to serve Him, and another loves only to serve himself. He will see that one has laid the foundation for a free, loving life of service on high, and that the other despises such a life, and must be brought to usefulness through constraint, or he will do harm wherever he is.

Thus of those who have awaked, as it were, at these times of judgment, there have been two classes, and only the unerring decision of Divine law could separate and adjudge them.

Some, oppressed long by scheming foes, being sincere in heart, are delivered, and rise to everlasting life; but others, to the shame of having their deceits exposed, and the sheep's clothing removed from their wolfish natures, while "they that be wise shine as the brightness of the firmament, and they that turn many to righteousness as the stars forever and ever."

One more point must be touched upon. This gathering of great numbers till the Lord interposes to break the power of those who rule over them, and hold them down, is not a condition to which men of this day are to look forward. They are becoming freer every day. The influences which keep them in one mass, subject to a human lord, are passing away. Babylon *is* fallen. By her sorceries were all nations deceived, but now she hath been judged. When one passes now into the other life, he does not pass from a religious serfdom to a similar state, but from freedom to freedom, and so he can soon proceed to his own place.

Under the working of Divine Order, his real

character soon manifests itself, and well is it for him if he can receive the saying, "Blessed are they that do His commandments, that they may have right to the tree of life, and may enter in through the gates into the city"; for this is the promise and privilege of the present age above all that have preceded.

Now is seen what the text and other such words mean. They literally describe the event in the other world. They figuratively describe the occurrence in this world of a judgment which the Lord would work and did work, raising from the lower parts of the world of spirits those who would follow Him, and exposing the true character of those who made righteousness only a pretence.

Men, in an important sense, judge themselves, determine their own future, and lay the foundations of their own spiritual after-life. Daily they wake to everlasting life or to shame. Daily they separate their thoughts and deeds, and can, if they will, exalt what is worthy to its true place, and put down as unworthy that which is shameful in the sight of the Lord and the angels.

Men can largely foresee their own future, and can prepare themselves for it. For they know that the Infinite Father has sent every one to do good work, to chasten his spirit, and to come some time to dwell on high. Only extreme and persevering perverseness can jeopardize that heavenly destiny. For the Lord's sake, for the sake of those who await them there, and of those who are with them here, may they so live in patience and uprightness that day unto day, under the Lord's guidance, they may wake to everlasting life!

THE LORD'S RESURRECTION.

"Whither I go ye know, and the way ye know."—JOHN xiv. 4.

THE festival of Easter means more or less to mankind according to the fulness or feebleness of perception anywhere of the event itself and of its bearing upon ordinary life. The man of science and nothing else, who admits as true only what he knows by touch, or sight, or taste, can enter but feebly into the common joy over an event which has indeed no force to one who doubts the existence of the other world.

To him also who is led to believe that all the Gospel story has but a thread of truth running through a warp made up of the errors of enthusiastic disciples, much doubt must mingle with his rejoicing.

There are also those who regard the resurrection

of men as in the far future, and so cannot draw from the Lord's experience direct lessons of life and death'; and there is a very large class, not included in the others, and consisting of those who wish to be made clear on the subject and have no prejudices in the matter, but are in some confusion when they came to apply to ordinary life what happened with the Lord. They would ask, "What became of His body?" "If He rose with His earthly body, what is the reason that we should not expect to have ours rise some time?" "But if He rose with His earthly body, why did they not know Him at once? and how did He enter when the doors were shut?"

These and similar questions, arising in the mind when the Lord's resurrection is spoken of, show a willingness to be made clear, if a wholly reasonable view can be presented.

But there is still another class,— of those who know about the Lord and the other world, and know how to draw the truth from the Lord's experience, having no other difficulty than belongs to finite minds. There is, of course, the impossibility of fully comprehending in all its depth of meaning the event of the resurrection, just as is the case with attempting a complete comprehension of anything Divine and infinite. But this class has no difficulty in seeing in their Lord's resurrection the promise of their own, and the means of its accomplishment.

In other words, when one speaks of having no difficulty with the Lord's words, or His acts, or His resurrection, he does not take the attitude of saying that his mind matches the Divine mind, and that his wisdom is infinite; but simply, that, so far as the words or acts of the Lord bear upon his own life and thought, he is able by the Divine mercy to see, and to see clearly. With such, the Lord's words are not dark, His acts are not mere wonders, nor is the manner of His resurrection a mystery; and such a nearness and fulness of view are, the New-Churchman believes, just what the Lord in His infinite goodness would have all men enjoy.

Let the great subject of the Lord's death and resurrection be taken up one point at a time.

I. The Lord died, and though all may have seen death and become familiar with it, His death will be found to be full of instruction. He went very calmly to die. The very painful manner of His death, more painful than men can conceive of, and more painful than men would have patience to endure for the sake of others, was met in a spirit which showed not the least uncertainty as to the future. "I lay down my life that I may take it again," He said to the disciples. And on the last night He said, " Peace I leave with you, my peace I give unto you"; "I go that I may prepare a place for you." And in the prayer which followed He said, "I have glorified Thee on the earth, I have finished the work which thou gavest me to do. And now come I to thee, and these things I speak in the world that they might have my joy fulfilled in themselves."

As men ponder these and similar words, spoken while Roman soldiers stood in their armor, or were already on their way to take Him, are they not moved with shame as they recall times of dread of death? or perhaps reflect that all their days are overclouded simply because they have to die, it may be in their easy beds, when He, before a death so agonizing, was as calm as heaven?

This is one of the lessons of the Lord's death.

II. But let no one fail to notice that His peace in those hours of torture was due to more than a full trust that all would be well. This is an excellent feeling if one can do no better, but, with the Lord, there was the clearest knowledge of the other life.

This was always a part of His speech about going away: "In my Father's house are many mansions. I go that I may prepare a place for you; and if I go and prepare a place for you, I will come again, and receive you unto myself, that where I am ye may be also." Let no one in these days, when the Divine Mercy has made very plain the contents of the Holy Word, live in this life ignorant of the other. Let no one make his will as if, in turning over his property, he terminated his life; but rather as one who lays aside his earthly blessings for the sake of receiving heavenly ones.

"If we could know about the other life, we should be happy," all Christendom is saying; and lo, all it needs to know is written where he who runs may read.

III. It is important to notice that the *manner* of the Lord's death, though surrounded by such hostile and unholy influences, was as gentle as any could ask for themselves. He simply "gave up the ghost," or, as would be said in modern English, "He gave out His breath," or "ceased to breathe." Who that has stood by the bedside of one near death has not been deeply moved by the gently advancing unconsciousness, the breathing less and less deep, the utter stillness of the frame, till at last the breath goes out, and comes in no more, and the body, after, perhaps, its eighty years of life, is at rest?

So it was with the Lord. Much sooner than usually happened with a crucified person, as the day drew to its close, with a last word spoken to Mary, "Behold thy son," and to John, "Behold thy mother," He said, "Father, into thy hands I commend my spirit; and having said thus, He gave up the ghost." And when the soldiers came to kill Him and the other two, lest the Sabbath should begin at evening with them unburied, they "came to Jesus and saw that He was dead already."

IV. In regard to the time which now followed, it is necessary to do scarcely more than to call attention to the fact that at death all pass into a sleep. "Our friend Lazarus sleepeth. I go that I may awake him out of sleep," our Lord said when Lazarus died. The fact that to die is to go to sleep, has been so clearly seen, that men have always so spoken of it.

When Stephen died under the attack of the foes of Christianity, he was upon his knees praying, "Lord, lay not this sin to their charge; and when he had said this he fell asleep." (ACTS vii. 60.)

The quiet sinking into sleep, when one's body is exhausted with disease, or fatally injured in any way, must be delightful beyond present conception; but many, who have been very near death, have told how a sweet peace overspread the soul; and how the presence of those gone before lulled the mind to rest.

Remember Hood's beautiful picture of the death-bed:—

> "We watched her breathing through the night,
>   Her breathing soft and low,
> As in her breast the wave of life
>   Kept heaving to and fro.
>
> Our very hopes belied our fears,
>   Our fears our hopes belied;
> We thought her dying when she slept,
>   And sleeping when she died.
>
> For when the morn came dim and sad,
>   And chill with early showers,
> Her quiet eyelids closed — she had
>   Another morn than ours."

V. The Lord's body, bearing the mark of the nails and the wound of the soldier's spear, was laid in a grave, or rather in a rock-hewn tomb. Here the thought presents itself that much of the fear of death is due to two causes, of which one is the dread that one may have some consciousness when his body is laid in the ground, and the other is that he must enter the other world alone.

Both these fears are like fears of ghosts, that is, wholly groundless. Under the old idea that the body is to be resumed some time, there might be a fear of retaining some sort of connection with the buried thing, but there is no reason for thinking so. Every one has noticed that, within a short time after death, generally by the third day, the expression of the face changes and loses all appearance of connection with the spirit. When the Egyptians spoke of knowing when their friends were carrying on their funerals, they did not mean that they would hear the songs in their old bodies, but from the spiritual world, as their words plainly show.

So as to the other cause of dread, namely, as to entering the other world alone. This, too, is wholly groundless and unworthy. If men come into it by awaking out of sleep, which follows, of course, from the fact that dying is going to sleep, the question simply is, Do they awake alone and unattended, or otherwise?

The answer to this question is that, as, when one comes into this world he is received by those who love him, so, when he enters the other, in the most gentle manner he will wake to find himself attended.

On the third day, but in reality within forty hours after our Lord's death, the two angels, seen to sit at the head and feet where His body had been laid, showed that the angelic attendance, which is provided during the earthly life, is continued also to the time of passing from this life to the other. The reason that the third day is the day of resurrection is, that it marks a sufficient period of transition and of separation of the soul from the body. Moreover, the number three, which is that of Divine and human completeness, properly applies to the completion of the state called death.

VI. Now comes a point needing some care.

The Lord rose on the third day; that is, on that day He was again with His disciples. There was a difference, however, for now He was with them when they had the doors shut, and henceforth He was seen at Jerusalem, or Emmaus, or at the Sea of Galilee, or at Bethany, only as He made Himself known. In other words, He had risen above the control of physical laws, and was to be seen only by spiritual eyes. For the same reason men do not now see Him with their bodily eyes.

That this change was in harmony with the great law of life, there can be no doubt. After death, men are spirits. As it was with Abraham, Isaac, and Jacob, of whom He spoke to rebuke the Sadducees, as with Moses and Elias seen at the time of the Transfiguration, as with the fellow-disciple seen by John when in the spirit, and as with the great multitude out of all nations and kindreds, so do all, when they die, enter a spiritual state.

The reality of that world may not seem clear to those who are accustomed to think of it as a mere shadow of this; but if one reflects that this is rather the shadow of that, that there the eternal life has its seat, and here only the temporal one, he will be able to view as actually true the descriptions of the other world found in the Sacred Scriptures.

But here the question arises, "Did not the Lord take up His earthly body, and are not we to take our earthly bodies?" This is best answered by the simple facts. In the tomb where the Lord had lain, was found only grave-clothing; in the graves in which men are laid, are found invariably earthly bodies going back to earth. This settles the matter. The Lord's resurrection did go beyond that of men in one respect. He took His body, they leave theirs. He did not, of course, take a body weakened and dead, but He took His glorified form which, while it was not excluded by doors of wood or stone, still might show the prints of the nails.

And there is a reason here which makes all plain. Man is to go to the other world and dwell there. The Lord is not to go to the other world and dwell there only, but to be in *all* degrees of life. His redemption as a *final* work depended upon this. He must be with men on earth always, and therefore He retained the natural with the spiritual, while men put off the natural.

And no confusion arises here unless one tries to make out that because, as the Saviour of men of all ages, He retained the natural in a glorified state, so all men must do it. Not at all. They are here to prepare for the future state. Some time they die, and enter upon it. Thus the fact that their earthly bodies moulder to dust, does not militate against the fact that the Lord's tomb was empty on the third day.

The lessons of the Lord's resurrection are,— calmness in view of death, perception of its nature as a painless sleep, knowledge of the attendance of angels, and expectation of awaking in their presence to the higher life. The fact that the Lord rose as to the body in a manner transcending the ordinary withdrawal from the material body, is seen to cause no confusion of thought, for only so could He be the Divine Saviour. So He said calmly, "Whither I go ye know, and the way ye know."

REUNION ON HIGH.

" Gathered to his people."— GEN. xlix. 29.

THE long life of Jacob drew to its close. The physical frame which had borne him, many years before, on that journey in which heaven was opened so that he saw the angels ascending and descending; which had enabled him to endure a service of twenty-one years with his kinsman, Laban; and which had, in its old age, still retained vigor sufficient to bear him down to Egypt to recover the long-lost son,—this frame, once so strong, was now approaching its dissolution.

Knowing this, the patriarch gathered together his children and children's children, and solemnly prophesied their future. Zebulon would dwell by the sea. Issachar would become a servant of tribute. Joseph would be like a fruitful bough by a well. So having done, the last words were to be spoken, and in a majestic manner he ended his speech. Thus the account runs,

" Every one according to his blessing, he blessed them: And he charged them, and said, 'I am to be gathered unto my people. Bury me with my fathers in the cave that is in the field of Ephron the Hittite.' . . . And when Jacob had made an end of commanding his sons, he gathered up his feet into the bed, and yielded up the ghost, and was gathered unto his people."

He had said the last words, and there was nothing now to do except to compose his body for burial, and to return to his ancestors.

Precisely the same expression,— "gathered to his people,"— is used of the deaths of Abraham, Isaac, and Ishmael, and was evidently a customary phrase for expressing that which is commonly called death.

Just what was understood in Jacob's day by this expression would be an interesting subject of inquiry, but it would be a question of history rather than of religion. It might be found that, while the Jews of the Lord's time had no idea of the hereafter, yet that sixty generations before, when Abraham lived, there was some knowledge of the subject,— a knowledge which, however, was ignorance when compared with what had been known before. Out of a very ancient time the phrase in question must have come, and of its use there can be no doubt.

Was Jacob indeed restored to his father and friends? Did Isaac return to his kindred, and to Rebekah? Was Abraham gathered to his own?

In considering this subject, all must confess that a few years have made a vast difference in the opinions of people upon this and kindred topics. Many can remember when the question, "are we restored to our friends by death?"—would have been regarded as unanswerable. A wide line was drawn between those having faith and those having none. On the one side was promise of joy, on the other promise of torment; and this was all. There might be no room hereafter for honesty nor industry nor even for human friendship. And the hereafter itself was not the next state of existence, but one next succeeding a long waiting for the judgment day.

Now, however, in many quarters, this is changed. The creeds still stand, and still declare those doctrines, the names of which are election, reprobation, and salvation by faith alone, but they stand like the deserted columns of some ancient temple from which priest and people have departed. The builders would not pull down the structure they had raised, and they left it to itself. So with the theology of two generations ago. It was then the mighty building which strong minds had erected. To-day it stands, but is no longer pointed to with the old pride.

Men are coming now to believe in an immediate resurrection, and that hereafter, as here, "the tree will be known by its fruits." They do not speak at the tomb of an endless slumber, but of a new life. They do not say, "he is dead, and awaits, in the grave, the judgment day;" but they say, "he is not here, he is risen."

The question to be pondered is this,— is the future life a reunion, as well as a reawakening? It is perfectly right to consider it. Indeed, it *must* be considered. The event of death is often occurring, and all have a right to ask whether the sadness so often falling upon them is temporal or eternal, whether they part to meet, or part and have no more of this world's friendships. As one has lamented : —

> "This is the burden of the heart,
> The burden that it always bore;
> We live to love, we meet to part;
> And part to meet on earth no more;
> We clasp each other to the heart,
> And part to meet on earth no more."

The poet utters the thought of the ages. Isaac at Abraham's death-scene, and Jacob at Isaac's, the children of Jacob receiving the last blessing, David crying "My son, Absalom, would God I had died for thee;" and myriads before and myriads since utter the same thought. In every language of earth it has been spoken, and spoken from the heart.

Has God heard, and how has he answered? Do men die to be gathered to their own, or to be parted forever?

The burden of proof in this matter is really upon those who would deny such re-assembling of friends. And it is put there by the simple fact of the friendships of this world. Humanity comes into the world, as a rule, amid most congenial surroundings, and makes friends from the very outset. This fact helps to predicate the other. The road which leads eastward to-day will lead thither to-morrow. What experience has proved to be the best way of treating a particular disease in twenty cases, reason leads all to try in the twenty-first.

If reason may not do so, if the continuity of Divine Order may not be taken for granted, nothing can be done. The physician will not dare to prescribe, lest yesterday's balm be to-day's poison. He will not dare to enter his vehicle, or to partake of food, or even to step out of his house, lest gravitation and cohesion may have perished.

So goes the argument heavenward. One may have ridden through many towns, and of all these has never found one which is a mere muster of strangers; but, on the contrary, in every place the people will be found banded together in the support of churches, and schools, and stores, and united still more closely in family relations. Ride a month, a year, a life-time, and the same will be seen. And this is sufficient.

If one would prove that friendship did not outlast the earthly life, he would have to show that cordial friendship was a thing accidental, unimportant, and only useful for a time. And this no man can show, for he knows that it is the mainspring of human progress, and divides the good from the brutal and the savage. Nay, the love which unites men with the Lord, knits them to each other; and the one would fall with the other, as trees fall when roots are severed.

While this is enough, it is not all. The Lord does not leave to human reason to work unaided, lest it err. And He has given much teaching on this point in the Holy Word, to which attention will now be given.

The phrase employed by the patriarchs has been noticed. It implies all. Found in the Holy Word, it promises all. It might well be on men's lips when they fade and when they die: "I am gathered to my people."

Moreover, David fasted and wept while his child lived; but when he perceived that it was dead, he washed his face and worshipped God. "For," said he, "while the child was yet alive, I fasted and wept: for I said, Who can tell whether God will be gracious to me, that the child may live? But now he is dead, wherefore should I fast? Can I bring him back again? I shall go to him, but he shall not return to me." So should all say, believing in the reunion hereafter, and in the need of preparing for it.

The tenderest friendship spoken of in Scripture is that of the Lord and His disciples. That He laid down His life for them and other men, and otherwise exhibited the fulness of the Divine

Love, is known. It is true, on the other hand, that the disciples hardly believed in Him, that at the last trial they forsook Him, and that they were infinitely His inferiors. Yet He loved them, and they Him. And the tie was not to break, nor would the separation be perpetual. "I go to prepare a place for you; and if I go and prepare a place for you, I will come again and receive you unto myself; *that where I am ye may be also.*" "Father, I will that they also whom thou hast given me be *with me where I am.*"

And He left with them and their successors full faith that they would finally be together with Him. Thus Paul wrote to the Thessalonians, "God hath not appointed us to wrath, but to obtain salvation by our Lord Jesus Christ, who died for us, that whether we wake or sleep, *we should live together with Him.*"

Of that blessed reunion of the disciples with their Master, a glimpse is given in the closing portions of the Gospels. He had died, and had risen again. They were thinking Him lost, and were trembling in a hiding place. Then He made Himself known, saying, "Peace be unto you." Thomas doubted, not having been present at first, but he soon believed, and cried out in joy and reverence, "My Lord and my God."

One more glimpse at the view as seen from the other side. In the Book of Revelation it is said that an angel showed to John the great city, and that John fell at his feet to worship him. But he prevented it, saying, "I am thy fellow-servant, and of thy brethren the prophets." A stranger was not sent, nor one of a different character, but a fellow-worker, a close sympathizer.

There are means to go much beyond this, but let this suffice. One caution, however, is to be made lest a vital principle underlying the whole matter should be overlooked. If friendships for good people are founded, not upon the good that is in them, but upon mere accidents of body or possession only, they have no abiding principle. Hereafter, nothing will be hidden. Each will show his dislike of another's honesty, or humility, or faith, and this will put a barrier between them. Friendships founded on a greater or less degree of common aim and common love are those which will last—friendships which seek good, not evil, and which seek the benefit, not the destruction, of others. Such only, to be sure, are real and true, but those of another sort are often seen.

It was not by accident that Peter, and James, and the rest were chosen, but by the design of Infinite Wisdom. It was not by accident that any are born of one nation, and state, and family, but of the same design. On this all should rest. The bands, grown strong in the companionship of years, are not to be rudely snapped, save as any do it by their own recklessness.

When children become of age they should look to the Lord for guidance, and their parents should cease to exercise authority over them; but they should still be the intimate friends of their children, having an accurate knowledge of their characters, and being as desirous as ever to assist them. Brothers and sisters, too, were given for a wise purpose, and this can be subserved by prolonging the tie beyond childhood.

Like the patriarchs, men of to-day are to be gathered to their people; unless they so affect their lives with evil as to prevent a union hereafter with the good. Then they will find new friends, but of another sort. The poor prodigal left his friends to seek others. He found, and was no longer an honored son; he became a slave and a swineherd. But he came to himself, and the same kind friend, his father, received him again with joy. May all departures from true friends result only in perceiving the desirableness of returning, that so all may find their own both here and hereafter.

The question as to the *recognition* of friends, which many ask with some anxiety, is not one requiring so full a treatment as they may suppose. To be in doubt upon the subject is to be in an obscurity which simple trust in the Lord will illumine. For to suppose that there is any impossibility or even difficulty in recognizing friends on high is to suppose that the Divine Love has failed in an important part of its work of blessing mankind. And to have a firm trust in the Lord is to be sure that He who doeth all things well will not leave men when they shall have gone hence to look upon those they once knew, and hesitate and fear to address them.

Note, however, that while the spiritual body may not have precisely the countenance of the earthly,— for sickness, age, or weariness will not mar the face hereafter,— yet that the *character*, which gives the light to the eyes, the grace to the smile, and the individuality to the whole contour, will remain, and will have perfect manifestation in every part and movement of the spiritual body.

Men treasure in memory the face of dear ones, not as they were last seen in death, but as they were in health and joyful energy. This recollection itself prevents them from disappointment through expecting to recognize the glorified by any marks which care or suffering may have made, and which resurrection will have taken away.

But it should be remembered that it will not be left for two to approach each other and scrutinize countenances. The mind of the departing is filled with thoughts of those gone before. They are, as it were, about his bedside. When he wakes, therefore, and finds them present, all anxiety as to recognizing them, if ever it was felt, is forgotten.

Again, those of the other side, awaiting the coming of a loved one, would leave him no time to doubt, by making themselves instantly known. Said one not long since, "My mother, who died years ago, seems of late always by me. I can think of nothing else. What does it mean?" He soon learned what it meant, when, with what seemed a sudden illness, he was taken hence.

Perhaps the doubt as to recognition may have some ground in what occurred with our Lord after His resurrection, when neither Mary at the tomb nor the two disciples upon the way to Emmaus knew Him at first. But this would be a false inference. The Lord could then be seen only by the spiritual sight, and it was for good reason that

He did not at once give a full recognition of Himself to those still in the flesh. Had they passed, however, into the other life, would they not have known Him even more certainly than the evil spirit who said, "I know Thee who thou art?"

> "Alas for him who never sees
> The sun shine through his cypress trees;
> Who hopeless lays his dead away,
> Nor looks to see the breaking day
> Across the mournful marbles play;
> Who hath not learned, in hours of faith,
> The truth to flesh and sense unknown,
> That life is ever lord of death,
> And love can never lose its own."

So believing, we can say with Paul, that "whether we wake or sleep, we shall live together with Him," — gathered to our people and to Him, and God shall wipe away all tears from our eyes.

THE BIBLE IN HEAVEN.

"Forever, O Lord, thy Word is settled in heaven." — PSALM cxix. 89.

THE Bible has held a high place in the hearts of millions of people who have found their light and consolation therein, in the minds of thousands who have suffered persecution rather than surrender it to the fires kindled by Romish priests, and in the thoughts of millions now, an increasing number in foreign lands, if not in our own, who look to it for guidance, encouragement, and warning, and who are never disappointed.

There are, to be sure, disquieting suggestions, lately brought to view, to the general effect that the Books of Moses were fraudulently produced, long after the times they describe, for temporary purposes of priestly aggrandizement, and that the Gospels had their origin long after the events they narrate, and when all means of attaining historic accuracy were lost.

In reply to these allegations, it would be easy to show their unreasonableness, and their demand that mere credulity should take the place of rational faith. Just as to that theory of the creation of the universe which sets aside the Creator and His plan, men are obliged to assent, if at all, against every rational consideration; so here they are compelled to suppose that a gigantic imagination has wrought where reason would say that it finds a record of actual occurrences.

If one should come and say to-day, "There may have been a George Washington somewhere, but the idea that he was the father of his country, was simply imagined by the historians, and the fact of a revolution in which he earned this title, is wholly doubtful," the answer would probably be made, "I cannot be so credulous as to believe you against all the facts, of which the very existence of the American nation is chief." And so it might be said of Christianity and Judaism, that their very existence is irrefutable evidence of their having had the source their records describe.

Such replies, with consideration also of the plain facts that the Bible is spiritual and Divine light, illuminating with a foresight all its own the things not within the range of human foreknowledge, sufficiently vindicate the Book as a guide in the present life, but they do not touch the supreme point, which is the existence of a deeper meaning in this Book, indicating at once its place above human compositions, and showing how it is found and read in heaven.

This is a point which should have interest far beyond its value as a matter of argument in the question of the authenticity of the Word.

One and another go out of this life, resigning earthly cares which have been well performed, and passing on to the restful life on high. All circles are sure to be broken within a short time, and the Lord alone knows who will be the first to go. Men, therefore, seek not only to be prepared in spirit for such a change, and to do all they now do as if it were their last duty on earth, but they also naturally think how the future life will be ordered, and what of home it will furnish.

This Bible they love, if it be there, will help to make the other life a home. If it be not found there, if, like a dictionary or an atlas, its use terminates with this life,— if, in fact, they have then to learn a new religion from new oracles, they will at the least lose a great treasure. It may be a real world; friends may be there; but this is not enough for those who have come to lean upon this sacred and unfailing staff. They want to know that the "Word is settled in heaven."

In making plain that it is there, one might proceed in two ways. He might go to the Word itself and see that it says this of itself, and elsewhere refers to itself as known in heaven,— as when angels came to men to cite its prophecies and indicate their fulfilment; or one might look at it in its own nature and see that it rises to the plane of the immortal life, and that, as a man has within his body an immortal spirit, so this book has within its literal meaning one which is such as the angels would read and delight in.

In order to consider this latter suggestion, it is necessary first to note what change of thought occurs with one who leaves this world.

When a person has left the natural body, he is in a spiritual body, and this has organs of sense, so that he sees, hears, and touches. But these organs, like the rest of his body, are spiritual. He therefore does not hear what is said on earth, nor see what is done there, as they of the earth do not know what is doing in heaven through sensuous knowledge.

The plain effect of this change from natural sights and sounds to spiritual sights and sounds, is to lay away into quiescence the memory of the sights and sounds of this world, and to lift the thought above natural objects. Those who go out from this life cease to concern themselves about the bodies and bodily affairs of those left behind, and rise to be concerned only about the working of their minds in regard to the most essential things. In the first state after death there is connection with all the thoughts of those who remain, but those who have become angels then concern themselves, with loving care and protection, only about the deeper purposes and affections.

They know not the particular work men are doing so much as the spirit in which they do it. They are concerned not to know how much wealth they accumulate, or what new clothes they procure, but they dwell near to the hearts of men, and feel their essential emotions.

To such persons, so raised in thought as not to heed earthly sights and sounds, a Scripture wholly about this earth would lose its power. Whatever it might have been to them once, if it continued on the level they formerly occupied, it would no longer give spiritual quickening to their thoughts. It is not meant to assert that the Word in its literal meaning is wholly such as to be called earthly, but it is clear that if it be partly so, the remark holds true.

Angels have no longer to do with Egypt, with

Babylon, nor with Jerusalem; and any reference to them in their Bibles would be dark. So would it be with all references to earthly towns or earthly acts, such as planting the ground, or carrying on worship by sacrifices, or vestments, or erecting temples.

The question then is, Is the Word capable of transfer to heaven? Can it lay off its garment of earthly history and scenery, and remain with those who go into the world of spirit? If *yes* can be intelligently answered to this question, the Divineness of the Word, however it may outwardly partake of Jewish thought, is forever established. Such answer must of course be given and received in freedom and reason. Not otherwise can true faith be founded or increased.

But the question, Is there an inner meaning in the Holy Word, one above earthly persons and places? hardly needs argument. The outer is so transparent that the inner is often brought to view. All through the history of Christianity an inner meaning has been known, or at least felt. "Which things are an allegory," said Paul, of the story of Abraham. Among the Christian Fathers, Origen, the most voluminous of the Fathers in the interpretation of Scripture, dwelt much on the same thought, and so explained, or sought to explain, the incidents of the Mosaic history, discerning clearly, for instance, that leprosy was a type of spiritual uncleanness, and that all the laws in regard to it had a bearing on the men of his day.

This too was dimly seen by a class commonly called mystics, who formed a line extending down to a recent date. They did not have the perfect rule of interpretation, but they clearly perceived that our Lord's words bore a double significance, that Rome might be the Scriptural Babylon, and that the destruction of the world might mean the end of the Church in corruption.

Reverent scholars at the present time, studying the use of symbols among ancient nations, are led to see that the same symbols introduced into the Holy Word must also bear interpretation. The Garden of Eden, for instance, with its two trees,

—the one good, the other dangerous,—its serpent, and its cherubim at the gate, is seen to be in the Word, as in the traditions of various nations, a symbolic account; only here, under Divine inspiration, it correctly assigns the cause of the Fall to man's abuse of his free agency.

Every commentary of any standing contains teaching about symbolism, especially when treating of the prophetic portions of the Word.

The difference between this historic belief and the one held in the New Church is only one of degree. While others are sure that they see a deeper meaning here and there, some see it all the way. They are led upon careful investigation to believe that, after a long, pure life of study into such things as prepared the way, Swedenborg was led to see the fact that a connected spiritual meaning runs through the Word, which, by a simple principle of interpretation, may be brought forth to the devout mind.

This is, by the way, the course of progress in all knowledge. A principle like that of the interrelation of the heavenly bodies is first dimly seen, and assertions are made by various astronomers, causing gradual increase of knowledge, till, at length, in His own time, the Lord raises up a man like La Place, who brings out the laws of the whole system, and shows at once its unity and its Divine authorship.

And so, in regard to the Word, did reverent men point out its transparent places till it pleased the Lord to give further light, and to show how the Word has an inmost as well as an outmost, and how it is in heaven as well as on earth.

This general thought, once seen, is perfectly clear, and yet men could not see it in its strength till they were taught. Here is the Word, and here are human souls. As was above explained, these souls are to pass above this earthly plane of life, and its sights and sounds, and are to lose their interest in them, but keep and deepen their interest in what with them is spiritual. When they have made this change, they will find the Word still a well of water of life.

As read in heaven, it is the same book; but, instead of the names of places and people, it speaks of spiritual things. Egypt, Canaan, Assyria, are not read there, but instead the regions of the mind. Wars with Philistines are not mentioned there, but combats with false teachings. The achievements of kings become the successes of the soul in the progress upward, and the crimes of men mentioned here relate the dangers of the soul.

Let it be noticed, that, when only a single part of speech receives this change, when only the nouns give place to their heavenly corresponding realities, the Word, wonderful to say, has risen a whole degree in the ascent of wisdom, and enthroned itself in heaven.

These symbols, moreover, are not arbitrary signs which must be learned one by one, as a man would learn the words of an unknown tongue, but they are the very order of the universe, by which every material object has its spiritual original, which is the means of its creation and of the preservation of its existence.

For instance, the Holy City, New Jerusalem, is a representative of the Church on earth, because a heavenly city is a collection of people of the Church, that is, of angels. And as everything surrounding them there answers to their hearts, so, when the same thing is described in the Holy Word in earthly language, we can read prophecies and lessons as to the Church among men, and can find them in every word as to wall, or gates, or street.

Some of the imagery of the Word is of infernal origin, such as the horrible beasts which sought to destroy; but here the principle of interpretation is the same, namely, to change the nouns to what they signify, and read of things spiritual.

Journeys then become progressions in wisdom and love, and all the march of the Israelites is the story of regeneration, while the story of their conquest of the land of Canaan becomes that of the acquisition of the heavenly powers and blessings which the Lord designs for all, if they will do their part.

After this, it will not surprise any one to be told that not only has the Word this spiritual meaning, but that it rises still higher, and treats of our Lord himself. Not only does the Exodus, for example, describe the course of a regenerating soul, but it also tells, when understood in a still deeper meaning, how the Lord glorified His Humanity, and so became the King of kings. It does this because there is a correspondence not only between matter and spirit, but between spirit and what is higher and Divine.

And it is scarcely necessary to add that a knowledge of the spiritual character of the Word does not at all diminish one's love of the letter. For this is the basis of all the rest. Hebraistic it may be and must be in its expressions; it may speak thus of things like Divine wrath, which have only an apparent and not a real existence; it may allude to crimes which can fill one only with horror; but it is still the Word of God. And in its more transparent places men can see its beauty and its power.

In studying it, however, the mind should not

dwell upon its outward meaning in ignorance or neglect of the inward; but, as one would treat men remembering their immortal souls, so here he would seek for "the spirit and the life," and will then surely find it.

Going hence, men may not take their earthly possessions, but they shall not part with the Bible. They should not cling now too closely to what is earthly, but they may cling to this. In the life beyond they may forget their fields, but they shall not forget their Bible, and in the light of the countenance of our Lord may they be permitted then, as now, to find here the daily lessons of truth. Blessed be thy mercy, O Lord, that "forever thy Word is settled in heaven," for "in thy Word do we hope."

THE HEAVENWARD CALL.

"Be of good comfort, rise; he calleth thee." — MARK x. 49.

HOLY Week commemorates the crowning acts of the Lord's life on earth. The mode of dating by the moon employed by the Jews has been preserved by them, and leaves no doubt that Christians celebrate these events on the very anniversaries of them. The passover, nineteen centuries ago, yes, thirty centuries ago, as now, occurred at the full moon, and the same moon which at her full in Holy Week mounts the heavens, looked down, long years ago, when a little company met and ate the Passover, then listened to words of comfort from their leader, who gave them a simple service of communion which they were to keep in remembrance of Him, and then passed with Him forth from the city gate and over into the Garden of Gethsemane. The same moon witnessed Him upon His knees in that garden, and the soldiers approaching with their arms. She stood over that fated city when He was tortured and unjustly tried; and when in early morning He was condemned to die in agony, she was sinking out of sight.

When she rose again on the next night, the crowd was still, the soldiers awestruck with what they had seen, and the cross unburdened. From her high station she watched the tomb, till again she descended into the West.

Once more she rose, and, ere she sank again, the tomb was empty, from the mourning faces the tears were wiped away, He had swallowed up death in victory.

The point to which attention is now called is an incident which happened a little before the events just referred to, when the Lord was on His way up to Jerusalem, and when He and His disciples were leaving the town of Jericho for the last part of the journey which would end in apparent defeat but real victory.

A man sat by the wayside, blind and poor. He had become well known to the people, by sitting near the gate on the road from this town Jericho to Jerusalem, and his only resource was to beg.

The suggestion that he in any way represents others will seem at first thought to have no foundation, but it is worthy of reflection.

Who knows all that he would like to know, or ought to know about the Lord, and the Word, and the duties of life here and hereafter? To how many does this book shine with the radiance of its spiritual meaning instead of being a mere history or a collection of sayings having the flavor of antiquity? Who is there that knows clearly and at once what is right in every case that arises to him? Who understands clearly about the other life? Especially, are there those who do not well know who the Lord is or what He is or where, who cannot see His hand in the circumstances which surround them or in the experiences which befall them, and who do not understand what the Redemption was and is; or are there those who cannot understand in what way and sense He was the manifestation of God?

Spiritual blindness! and that perhaps wide spread and of long standing. There is not one who can fail to see in himself something of ignorance; and when he looks out upon the world and hears the doubts going back and forth,—the denials of Divine facts, the honest declarations of ignorance,—he cannot fail to see an analogy between this blindness and that of the man of Jericho. Alas that a poet should say with truth of himself, sorrowing blindly for his friend:—

> "But what am I?
> An infant crying in the night:
> An infant crying for the light:
> And with no language but a cry."

This blindness or lack of understanding in respect to spiritual matters is not typified by the man of Jericho, if it be reckless of the consequences, and cries out, "I see, and what I do not see is not." So far as men make their lack of understanding the limit of knowledge, so far as they say to others "our horizon is the world's end," they are not in the attitude to be helped. Yet, incredible as it may seem, there is much of this, and it is just as if the blind Bartimaeus should cry out and say, "What do you say you see? One who can cure? A way up to Jerusalem? you are wholly mistaken, for I see nothing of the sort. What vain imagination, what superstition, my eyes are better, and the only good eyes; my place is higher than Jerusalem; your Saviour you only dream of!"

He was not such. He begged, because he *knew* himself miserable. Without sight he knew he was, and when he heard the others tell what they saw, he was not scornful, he was not angry, he listened and sought to know what they knew. His attitude perfectly represents an ignorance that is teachable, and therefore hopeful.

And he placed himself on the way to the Holy City! It was not by the path to the desert that he sat, thinking to go out there if he could. The road he lingered by ended at the Temple. The people who passed him were singing as they went, the songs of Zion, and he heard with longing.

It is the best position men can take so far as they are conscious of any obscurity of mind, or of any lack of nearness to the Lord. They gain nothing by concealing, they lose immeasurably by denying their need. Waiting patiently with ears intent, they will learn that all they need is at hand when some one says, "Jesus of Nazareth passeth by." They cannot call him Lord and Master at first; He is, to them, only Jesus of Nazareth, a character in history. And if they decide not to call to Him, He will pass by to-day and to-morrow and so on, and always be to them a mere character in history, the greatest of men, but not the Saviour.

But let them remember unto what they were made, by whom and with what wonderful skill, and let them not love their blindness, and say, "I see" when they grope in darkness. Nor let them delay. Let the angels speak through them, let the prayers for them of those who love them be heeded, let their cry go forth, "have mercy on me."

What was the answer? A rebuke. Not from Him, but from those who applauded Him to-day, and would throng the street to cry "crucify Him" ere the week closed.

There are places to-day in which this cry would be rebuked, or passed by as childish. The rebuke of the people was well meant, but it was heartless indeed. They wanted no pause for beggars. They "charged him that he should hold his peace."

What shall be done if the good purpose does not instantly meet with full response, if when men try to come to church they find the people cold, the minister not understanding their wants or even denying their good sense? There is but one answer. Heaven and earth must be moved to make them safe and happy. Theirs are immortal souls, fashioned by the Lord of the Universe, marred, it may be, by their own hands but not destroyed, groping blindly and feebly while the sun in heaven shines in all his strength. Let them remember that it is written "Before they call I will answer, and while they are yet speaking I will hear," and let them do right, as Bartimaeus did. "He cried the more a great deal, 'Thou son of David, have mercy on me.'"

There can be no failure where the purpose is strong; and, if it be a true purpose, misunderstandings will not break, but will only chasten it. They will cry out the more. Mark, that intense study is not the best way to reach the cure of ignorance about the Lord. If one but goes into his closet to the Lord, the Lord shows who He is and opens the eyes to see Him. Such is His power over all obstructing influences that they cannot oppose when He is before one in answer to his cry.

At the second appeal the Lord stood still, and commanded the man to be called. This is the opportunity of all, and joyfully the church should second it, saying, "Be of good comfort, rise; He calleth thee."

It is a solemn question for every one, minister

or layman, to answer to himself,— is this my answer to those of whose needs I learn? do I comfort them? do I exhort them? do I tell them of the Lord's call to them to come and be healed? Without attempting to answer for the past, let this duty of encouraging and of being encouraged be urged upon all.

"Be of good comfort." Are any in some sorrow, the means of assuagement are at hand. They may learn that those they deem lost are only gone before, that the errors they mourn may be repented of, that the doubts which trouble them are not of the Lord's sending, and are only phases of thought through which they can easily see their way if they make the attempt. The evils of the world are of men's making, the weaknesses of mankind are not a necessity and may be overcome. Approach once the Lord, and all will be in process of cure. "Be of good comfort."

But there is more than this. "Rise." This is indispensible. One must *move* in this matter. Human beings cannot be used as machinery. It was a sad mistake of the old theologians that some men were saved by irresistable grace and others condemned by unavoidable wrath. Men's destinies are in their own hands. The whole Scripture was set aside by this doctrine of unconditional election and reprobation. "Come unto me, all ye," is the bidding; "look unto me, and be ye saved all the ends of the earth." And the way to move is plain.

Rising means going up and away from whatever darkens or enfeebles. It is the effort to reform. It is yielding to the saving impulse of the Lord within. In all the decisions which arise to be made, it is choosing the better part. And this should be done because He calleth. Earnestly to seek salvation for one's own sake is not ennobling. The appeal to men to repent for fear they will suffer is not strong. Right is to be done because it is right. All are to pray as well for others as for themselves. They are to seek the Lord, not merely to obtain a token of His good-will, but to become in heart and mind and life the men and women

He intended them to be, strong, true, patient, affectionate.

To all this He calleth, not to mere bliss, not to eternal idle contemplation of one's own happiness and others' misery, but to earnest work in any calling, without worldly ambition, without over-indulgence of the body, with a noble love of the Master and the fellow-workers.

In a life of this sort there is progress. None seeks healing for the purpose of going back to stay where he was, but to leave that behind. He would see the other end of the road at the beginning of which he has lingered long. There is a Jericho here, the first stage of life. There is a Jerusalem there, the heavenly home. And men cannot see it without eyes.

It is a vital truth that Jericho is so low in the valley that no one can see Jerusalem. He who abides all his life at a great distance from the Lord, is preparing himself so to abide in the other life. If, on the other hand, he has sought to know the Lord for himself, has found Him, and has come to realize His presence day unto day, he dies and lives again *in His presence*, he will love to see Him, he will be with the Lord where He is, in the light of His countenance he will find peace.

This is all set down in the story. When he heard the call, Bartimaeus rose, casting away his garment, "and came to Jesus." He did that which clearly represents what all should do. Casting away the garment means a change of life,— the putting away of the tokens of misery for those of joy. Bartimaeus was to have a new calling, and a more worthy one; the rags of his begging he abandoned.

And he went to Jesus. It was but a step, but he must take it. All must go that step. All must elect *themselves* to grace. Being rational human beings, and not machines, they must act in freedom according to reason. There can be no persuading and no threatening. He sins who, in dealing with mature people, does not reason with them in regard to religious things. He cannot take this step for them. They must rise and go to Jesus; with the aid, the encouragement of others, but not by others' power, but by their own.

"And Jesus said unto him, Go thy way: thy faith hath made thee whole." This was the end he sought. It came to him without fail. The Lord's power is infinite. A very slight exercise of it made this man well, and makes myriads well. The Lord withholds it only for their sake; indeed He exerts so much of it as will keep them free to choose, as will prevent their being overwhelmed of evil, and as will turn them to Himself; but, out of His wise love for them, He does not add the grain more which would force them from their birthright as free agents. This He exercises only when they seek Him, and so act as of themselves. Then He "*pours* water upon him that is thirsty, and floods upon the dry ground." "Immediately he received his sight, and followed Jesus in the way." So he saw Jerusalem, that had long been blind. So the weakest may be strong to follow Him, the day-spring from on high which giveth light to them that sit in darkness and in the shadow of death.

It is the solemn question of the hour, Shall Holy Week close and leave one at Jericho? Shall all not go up with their Lord? If any are already outwardly united with them that seek to follow the Lord, let them make it a season of greater surrender of self to Him. If they are not outwardly united with them that go, shall they not reverently and joyfully receive His mark upon their foreheads and drink of the cup He drank of?

No one can answer these questions for another, nor can ministers answer for their people. As it is, pointing to the way which goeth up from all that is unworthy to what is glorious, from this present weakness to the kingdom prepared from the foundation of the world, one can only say to another, "Jesus of Nazareth passeth by; be of good comfort, rise; He calleth *thee*."

THE HEAVENLY PREPARATION.

"Like unto men that wait for their lord."—LUKE xii. 36.

IF it were now permitted to look upon those who have been removed from any community to the other life within the last few years, and to observe their present conditions and surroundings, it would be perceived that their situations were not alike.

Those who had been removed in infancy would be found to be in the charge of angels especially adapted to care for them, being those whose love of children was most earnest while they were in this world. There the children will be not only cared for, but instructed in wonderful ways, and they will receive all that they need to make them blessed forever.

Those too who had been taken hence when in childhood would also be seen to be in the hands of wise and loving guardians.

This is known because it is written, "It is not the will of your Father which is in heaven that one of these little ones should perish," and because it is said that "He is not the God of the dead, but of the living, for all live unto Him;" and true life, whether in this world or the next, implies progress in affection and intelligence.

In regard to those who had made the change of worlds in adult life, the general remark may be made that they all continue to live, for the Scripture applies the term everlasting to the evil as well as to the good; but it does not describe the same future as awaiting both evil and good.

Of those who have been taken, some may have been so thoroughly evil, so opposed to the principles of an orderly life set forth in the Ten Commandments, that it was necessary for them to be at once restrained from injuring others. Their quality may have been that of those who enjoy nothing but selfish gratification. Such people, if they are in business, care more to obtain the ruin of others than to advance themselves; and in social life their thought is of leading other people astray. Their pretended friendship lays a heavy hand upon those who come under their influence, and makes them subject to the stronger will. And when they go into the other life they seek to do likewise.

Such persons are rare, and some communities may not contain them. But if there were any among those now referred to, they soon after death made their quality manifest, and it would be necessary to put them into the company of others like them. Such would also be their own free choice, and they would be placed under restraint, as was necessary in this world, lest they should go on to grow worse, which can no longer be permitted them.

The good hereafter gladly perceive the control of the Heavenly Father; the evil do not acknowledge it gladly, but they do and must submit to it. "If I ascend up into heaven, thou art there; if I make my bed in hell, behold thou art there."

Besides these, there are in the class of those recently departed, undoubtedly a large proportion of people whose lives in this world were of a mixed quality. They may have felt kindly towards some, and vengefully towards others. They may have had some good habits and some evil ones. They may have been interested at times in learning truth of every degree, and at others they may have been worldly, and may have weakened rather than strengthened their minds.

If, when such were in this world, the question had been raised, Are you ready for the Lord to come, are you ready to go hence? they would have answered, No; we wish to get over this quarrel with a neighbor and become reconciled to all men. We wish to give up this vile habit of self-indulgence, and become all pure. We wish to cease to be foolish, and become truly wise and sensible. We wish to learn to love to be with good people, and to overcome our desire to be with evil people in evil places. We wish to be able to look on riches without envy, on beauty without impurity of thought, on afflictions submissively. No; we must not go now; all this and more we must do before we shall be ready to go where the hidden shall be revealed.

Yet they went, and went as they were; and the infinite love and wisdom of the Lord have been occupied since their departure, as before it, in seeking to bring them to be of one quality, not fond of the good to-day and of the evil to-morrow, nor of wisdom to-day and of foolishness to-morrow, but of one nature, that they may have some abiding-place, either among the blessed free or the pitied and restrained, as may be fitting for them.

At the present stage of human history, it needs but a glance to see that they are the large class, including the most of those who do not go to church at all, and all those who go from motives of fashion or curiosity.

They are not preparing for the Lord, nor are they making a continued effort to become prepared. Serious moments they have, especially when they are wrought upon by startling events, but they make at best only a temporary use of them. A while they turn to go onward, and presently linger, and look back, and anon are travelling downward again, forgetting that a wasted hour is an irrevocable hour.

In the same class, though far removed, are those who, while they make a general effort to be prepared, suffer themselves to indulge hard thoughts occasionally, without feeling sorry for doing so; or who, in business transactions, sometimes act or utter an untruth without repenting and making amends; or who indulge at rare intervals in what they know to be debasing, contenting themselves with the idea that it will not ruin them as it does others.

These are double people, and in the hereafter there can be no doubleness. There is no company of those who gladly do as the Lord wills three-fourths of the time, and insist upon doing according to their own evil desires one-fourth of the time. That vast class, when it goes hence, must divide. It is the teaching of the account of the sheep and goats, that all men, departing this life, must stand either upon the right hand or upon the left, every one receiving according to his neighborliness or unneighborliness.

What those who have departed in this half-prepared state may have endured ere they could lay aside forever the long-indulged one evil, or could sincerely repent of the habit of occasional and unmourned anger, or impurity, or profanity, no one knows; but all can see that to go into the other world, where good is good and evil evil, and to go with an affection for both, is to go unprepared.

Perfection the Lord does not expect, but He asks that not one moment of the earthly life be passed in indifference or in intentional sin.

Is there still another class? Were there any who were far removed from being of the first or evil sort, and who had done or tried to do their daily work in one great effort to be not of the double-minded? Not that they made their lives a selfish heaven-seeking, trying to hoard goodness as misers hoard gold; this would have defeated their object.

But there were, doubtless, some who realized

that the great purpose of the Lord in creating and preserving was to have them find their happiness in doing something as well as they could, and kindly and patiently. And suppose that in the progress of years they became so advanced upon this course that, if they thought in time, they would not do a wrong on any account, and, if they did not think, and failed to tell the truth or to be patient, they were sorry, and sought to make amends. And suppose that they learned to have a continual dependence upon the Lord, as a child upon its parents, and that they learned to set all their plans before Him, and to carry them out in consciousness of His presence. And suppose that the ruling desire of their lives came to be to know just what He would have them do, and to do it, or to suffer willingly for His sake and the sake of His children.

Thus they were single in purpose, and then were taken. Falling asleep, they knew not when the cord which bound them to the flesh was loosed, and they woke to find themselves in the peaceful company of the angels who had been expecting them.

Was there any need of further trial? Had *they* any struggle to make before they could go in with those whose heavenly lives were of gentleness and truth? Or could they come almost at once into the place provided? It is written that the King would say to those on His right hand, "Come, ye blessed of my Father, inherit the kingdom prepared for you from the foundation of the world."

It is written again of the great company seen on Mount Zion, "These are they who follow the Lamb withersoever He goeth; and in their mouth was found no guile, for they are without fault before the throne of God."

These are they who are described in the command,—for they are those who had obeyed its injunction,—"Let your loins be girded about, and your lights burning; and ye yourselves like unto men who wait for their lord when he will return from the wedding; that when he cometh and knocketh, they may open to him immediately."

These, and these only, are those who, not delaying for further preparation, could *open immediately*.

The Lord took His illustrations from the scenes and customs familiar to the people, and in this case from their wedding observances.

At such a time, there was no religious service, but the ceremony included a procession from the house of the bride to her new home. The groom made preparations for going with his friends to her house, and left orders with his servants to have all things ready for the feast which would take place on his arrival, and to watch his coming, that the doors might be thrown open at once when the procession arrived. Considerable delay might be caused by the distance to be traversed, or by other causes, and it would be impossible for the master to say when he would arrive. He could only say that it might be in the evening, or at midnight, or at the cock crowing (about three hours later), or in the morning, and that they were to remain awake till he came.

It is thus that the Lord does with all. His coming is intended to bring the end of watching, which may be sometimes long, and to inaugurate the life of the hereafter which, to those who are capable of true delight, will be like a feast for joyfulness.

But He does not say when He will come. It would not do for men to know, for then their preparation might either be done under sense of dread, or they might endeavor to prevent the event or to postpone it. He therefore does not let them know. Simply saying that He will surely come, and will come soon. He asks all to watch continually for Him.

People in the East wore and still wear loose garments, and before they can be ready to go out to meet the bridegroom, or to wait upon him at the feast, they must gather up their garments with a girdle. It was necessary, therefore, in order to be ready, that they should have their garments girded up before he knocked. Their lamps also, being small vessels into which a wick was laid, needed to be filled and lighted in due season.

Men's loins are girded about and their lights are burning, if they are doing their various duties in an honest, affectionate, wise way, in such a way indeed that the Lord's will is acknowledged; so that, if they should see Him looking upon them as they work, or should have their most valued friend with them all the time, they would not be confused.

The Lord sometimes comes without an instant's warning, or the last sickness may be such as prevents making further preparation,—and little *can* be made in an acute illness.

The only true way is to live as if one waited for the master to come back from the wedding, and expected at any moment to hear his knock, and stood ready to open immediately.

He comes in a sense every day. All opportunities of doing work, or of feeling kindly, or of learning wisdom, are soft knocks of His hand at the door of the heart, to the end that when we open He may enter and abide. If any be glad of such opportunities, they open, but if they neglect them, or act tardily and grudgingly, they are either servants rebellious, or servants dilatory and untrustworthy.

It is only by gladly accepting Him now that they are made ready to accept Him then. If they but half accept Him now, they are but half prepared to accept, and half inclined to reject Him then. If, which may God forbid, they utterly refuse to open to Him now, they will utterly refuse then, and must be brought to some usefulness by coercion.

There is no room to doubt as to the way which is most worthy of His children. The true way leads men to be much more helpful in this world, and it is for now and for ever the best for them.

That blessed state of loins girded and lights burning is well described in a poem: —

> "If I were told that I must die to-morrow,
>   That the next sun
> Which sinks should bear me past all fear and sorrow
>   For any one,
> All the fight fought, all the short journey through,
>   What should I do?

> I do not think that I should shrink or falter,
>   But just go on,
> Doing my work, nor change nor seek to alter
>   Aught that is gone;
> But rise, and move, and love, and smile, and pray,
>   For one more day.
> And lying down at night for a last sleeping,
>   Say in that ear
> Which hearkens ever, ' Lord, within Thy keeping
>   What should I fear?
> And when to-morrow brings Thee nearer still,
>   Do thou Thy will.'
> I might not sleep for awe; but peaceful, tender,
>   My soul would lie
> All the night long; and when the morning splendor
>   Flushed o'er the sky,
> I think that I could smile,— could calmly say,
>   It is His day."

When the Lord spake as He did, one had just come, saying, "Speak to my brother that he divide the inheritance with me." All stand in the presence of Him before whom the hereafter is present, yet they are apt to remember only this world's interests. They must not neglect them, but they must attend to them in full consciousness that He is even now on His way, and will soon come and say, "Render an account of thy stewardship."

"Blessed are those servants," it is written, "whom the Lord, when He cometh, shall find watching. . . . And if He shall come in the second watch or come in the third watch, and find them so, blessed are those servants. Be ye, therefore, ready also, for the Son of Man cometh at an hour when ye think not."

IN AFFLICTION.

"And I will cover thee with my hand while I pass by."—
Exodus xxxiii. 22.

THERE is no scene in all the history of Moses more pathetic than this. He had a longing to see the face of his God which words cannot express, yet he could not see it. He felt that there was a necessity that he should worship and proclaim a visible God, yet God remained invisible.

The Israelites had come to the mountains of Sinai, and had entered upon a sojourn there which lasted more than a year. Their leader had been summoned into the nearest mountain, and had ascended to learn the will of Him who had directed them to come hither. It was probable that now the object of the deliverance from Egypt would be more fully declared; and that Moses would learn how to extend his leadership.

IN AFFLICTION. 155

A complete code of laws was indeed made known, and after a stay of forty days, Moses returned to put into execution the commandments transmitted. But meanwhile the depravity of his people had overcome their new hopes. Ignorant of this God who had led them, they well knew the gods of Egypt. Doubtful as to the result of the stay of Moses in the mountain, they turned to their former reliance—a molten image.

Slowly descending with his servant Joshua, Moses could hear, before he could see, a tumult, and this soon declared its nature. A wild, brutal feast was going on. The people which he had left standing devoutly before the sacred mountain were at play. The leader cast the stone tablets from his hands, and ran in among them to expostulate and punish.

⸱ The punishment was direful, but not more than sufficient to curb the lawlessness of the people. The golden calf was broken up. The sons of Levi ran through the camp and slew many. A sudden contrition fell upon them, and the world has never known a people which could be more contrite for a time.

After this, some precautions were taken to obviate a second return to idolatry. Moses took his tent and pitched it in a remote place, and made it for the time the temple of God, and hither the people came with awe to what they supposed to be the nearer presence of God; while, over this tent, the pillar of bright cloud, dimly revealing the presence of the angels of God, abode like a crown of glory.

Thus it was when Moses ascended again, bearing with him two tablets to replace those which had come to him from heaven, and which he had broken,—a token that the people were too depraved to receive the law as it is in heaven. And as he went up, one thought seems to have been in his mind—his desire to see God. He probably believed that, had God made Himself distinctly visible to the people, the disaster might have been avoided. He undoubtedly felt within his own heart that weakness of faith which could easily be remedied by an actual sight of his God. So he prayed for it, and said, "I beseech thee, show me thy glory."

He did not say that he would go no farther without this proof, but he uttered a wish which all men have, and which has led many into idolatry. The heathen with their images, the Romanist with his crucifix, the Eastern Christian with his picture before which he daily bows, only show the desire of men for a visible God.

It was not so from the first, for men had had an inward sense of the presence of God, and had rested in it. They had needed no written commandments, for the law was in their hearts. They saw something of the Divine imaged forth in every object, and would not have been strengthened by seeing or touching the Divine. But later, when human thought had lowered itself, and had begun to hearken to other dictates than those of inward perception of right, written words of precept were necessary and were given, and men carved statues to remind them of the attributes of God.

Here however they did not stop, and at length the precepts were disobeyed, and mere superstitious worship of idols grew out of their respect for symbolic forms.

Then, as a temporary gift, came Judaism,—a ritual accommodated to the fallen nature of men, but embodying in its significance a true worship and life. It was the life of the angels of heaven brought down into a form suited to depraved men and women.

But now the state of men was such that, in the brief interval between leaving Egypt and obtaining at Sinai the plan of the new worship, they were likely to fall into gross practices. And Moses was not so much above the people that he could resist the craving for a visible object of worship. "I beseech thee," cried he, " show me thy glory."

What was the answer? He could see the glory only when it had passed. The time had not yet come for men to see God. Nearly fifteen hundred years must pass before the time should be fully ripe for the manifestation of God. Then, by means of a nature born of woman, the answer to Moses' prayer was given. No man had seen God at any time; but the only-begotten Son, who is in the bosom of the Father, He declared Him. Veiled as it were in a Galilean nature, the Infinite Love and Wisdom were made known, and, by a process of temptation and purification, that veil was made more and more transparent till it rent from top to bottom, and even doubting Thomas cried out, "My Lord and my God."

Some did not, some do not, see in the Lord the living God; but plainly He taught, "He that hath seen me hath seen the Father; How sayest thou then, Show us the Father?"

Until this Incarnation, God could not be seen. Except when He had come down in a form on which they could look, He was absolutely invisible. He might and did speak to the prophets through angels, but was not otherwise known. But when the Lord came, He was "the brightness of his glory, and the express image of his person."

What then could be given to Moses? Only to

see a bright cloud, the presence of angels partly visible, and to hear a voice proclaiming the character of God in immortal words. Standing, overcome with awe, in a cleft of the rock on the summit of the mountain, Moses saw, passing on, a radiance from which came a voice proclaiming, "The Lord, the Lord God, merciful and gracious, longsuffering, and abundant in goodness and truth, keeping mercy for thousands, forgiving iniquity and transgression and sin, and that will by no means clear the guilty; visiting the iniquity of the fathers upon the children and upon the children's children, unto the third and fourth generation."

Completely satisfied, at least for the time, with this manifestation of a glory not earthly, Moses made haste, and bowed his head towards the earth, and worshipped, and said, "If now I have found grace in thy sight, O Lord, let my Lord, I pray thee, go among us; for it is a stiffnecked people; and pardon our iniquity and our sin, and take us for thine inheritance."

Standing there in spirit with Moses, the Christian feels gratitude for the mercy which was granted the Israelite in giving him some idea of the Divine presence and glory, although the time for a full revelation of the Divine was still far distant; and, with Moses, he is led to recall his iniquities and sins, and to pray that, in spite of his manifest failings, he may be taken for God's inheritance, and may have some share in those rich blessings which "he hath prepared for him that waiteth for him."

One particular lesson may however be overlooked, if it be not mentioned while all look with close sympathy upon this scene, imagining the rocks of Sinai about them and the music of the movement of the angelic host.

This lesson is one for which every one has use every day, and without some knowledge of which very much of life is dark. Every one in a sense is in a cleft of the rock, every one sees the Lord *after* He has passed by.

When one reads in the biography of Swedenborg that, in later life, he realized that he had been led all the way by the Lord, so that the duties and trials of his life had been a preparation for the sublime privileges which fell to him, one does not think of this as necessarily an exceptional experience, but thinks of it as a common expression with old people who are good. They look back as one looks from a summit upon the path by which he ascended, and says, now I see all the way: that place where the climb was so steep, I see how much distance it saved; and that place where the trees were so thick, I see that it was the best place to pass, for on either hand the thicket was impenetrable; and that place where I thought ground lost, it was a bit of descent but it brought me round to that passable way when otherwise I could have gone no farther.

It is this lesson of the past which Mrs. Browning draws from when she says,—

> "O dreary life, we cry, O dreary life!
> And still the generations of the birds
> Sing through our sighing, and the flocks and herds.
> Serenely live while we are keeping strife

> With heaven's true purpose in us, as a knife
> Against which we may struggle. Ocean girds
> Unslackened the dry land : savannah swards
> Unweary sweep ; hills watch, unworn and rife,
> Meek leaves drop yearly from the forest trees,
> To show above the unwasted stars that pass
> In their old glory. O thou God of old !
> Grant me some smaller grace than comes to these,
> But so much patience as a blade of grass
> Grows by, contented, through the heat and cold."

If this be the lesson of life looked back upon, note with Moses that men cannot see the Divine Providence so well in its face. The future of the Divine plan in its near relation with any one is a book he has not read. Who, in his childhood, pondering why he was of this family and not of another, why his people went to one church and not to another, why this friend came often to the house, why the little duties, which are a full charge for children's strength, were imposed when he would rather play, why he had a certain teacher,—what child, pondering these things, can see more than that the good Father of all will sometime show him? And what parent can tell him more than that he will see in time? "What I do thou knowest not now, but thou shalt know hereafter," is the law of Providence. The Lord foresees, men do not. He covers them with the hand of His care till He has passed by.

The same thoughts come often to the minds of grown people. Why am I sick? cries one, brought to a pause in full career of usefulness, and having many plans for the future. Why am I sick, and so suddenly checked in all my work? Man cannot answer; the future must answer, and will answer, and will proclaim this Lord, whose hand now seems heavy, to be a Lord "merciful and gracious, long-suffering and abundant in goodness and truth."

Why, laments another, am I unfortunate while others prosper? What good can come of it? what mercy can be in it? He demands to know; he *will* know hereafter if he retains a teachable spirit, but he cannot so well see now.

In the affairs of communities and nations come

these times of being in the cleft of the rock. What means it? all were asking, when war came upon them. Every one asked his neighbor, and had answer that it meant pain,— pain in desolate homes, pain on bloody fields. What else it meant no man knew. God knew. In time men learned that the war had lessons of which they had not dreamed. Whirlwind, earthquake, and fire passed by before the nation smitten, and then a still, small voice said, "The Lord visiting the iniquity of the fathers upon the children and upon the children's children unto the third and fourth generation."

Times of trial, private, local, national, are not passed, and this lesson, therefore, all greatly need to remember. Fire comes, pestilence comes; and some doubt the mercy of God. By-and-by they see the meaning, and know what at first they could not know.

This is no general assertion, to be received only on faith. If any one doubts that he will ever look back upon his life, he does it against all fact and reason. The elders who so placidly spend their remaining days, are their minds idle? No. Are they fully concerned with present duties? No. They are pondering the past. Every day brings its reminiscences, giving much of happiness and little of pain; for memory has a healing process like a tree, and will not always show its wounds, if men give it help to heal them.

Some may pass suddenly into the other life, but it will not then be too late to look back. On the contrary they will then plainly find that the books of their lives speak of every word and deed, and that every day of wind, and storm, and sun are marked therein forever.

The failure now, or especially in old age, to recall what one wants to remember, is not a sign that memory is dying, but that the power of using it, as of using the hands, is lessened. The book is written in imperishable letters, and will reveal some day what has been forgotten now, and the mercy of the Father, who comforted and who disciplined, will gleam forth.

Why one knew this friend, why he had this

burden, why he was led to work in this employment, why he had these gifts, and these denials of what he sought for, will all be plain. He need not remember the date, the spot, the raiment, the weather. The memory of these will pass; but the thought, the deed, the effect for good or ill, these remain written in light.

> "Music, when soft voices die,
> Vibrates in the memory;
> Odors, when sweet violets sicken,
> Live within the sense they quicken."

And the lesson of it all is that though the Divine One had not in Israel's day made Himself visible to men, and though He did not show Himself to Moses, He did reveal His Providence and the way in which it deals with all. He passed by, He spake, He comforted, He vindicated His mercy.

God is now to be seen. With the inward eye, if any are near Him in spirit, they can see the risen Lord. His face, all radiant as upon the Mountain of Transfiguration, reveals infinite love and wisdom. None can ask for more than the fulfilment, now possible, of the promise, "They shall see His face, and His name shall be in their foreheads;" and if sometimes there is fear that He has forgotten, let there be faith that His children are safely covered by the shadow of His hand, and that in due time they will hear the voice, and see the purpose of "the Lord merciful and gracious."

AFTER AFFLICTION.

"A little while, and ye shall not see me; and again a little while, and ye shall see me, because I go to the Father."—JOHN xiv. 16.

SO often as death comes, it is common to combine with the act of burial a religious service. With reading from the Scriptures, remarks to mourning friends and prayer to the Father of Eternity, those who are bereaved are in some measure prepared to go forth, as becomes Christians, and to commit the body to the earth, while the thoughts are lifted to the higher world. This done, the most difficult task is still to be performed, and it is one for which the religious services may not fully have prepared one.

Those who have experienced this difficulty will not need to be told what it is. They will remember that the moment of their greatest suffering was when they returned to the home from which so much had been taken. A room about which their thoughts had gathered for months and perhaps years, towards which their careful steps had crept day after day to bear some offering of love to the sufferer, and in which the tenderest words had been whispered, is now empty. A care, deemed most precious and recently absorbing all their attention, is over forever. Suddenly, they feel an affliction more difficult to bear than all the rest,—the loss of the presence of the loved one.

While the body remained in their keeping, they could watch over it; even during the services, they still had its presence; but now this is gone, and they must learn to do without this object of love.

To those who have experienced this great trial, it does not seem strange that the Egyptians embalmed their dead and wrapped them in linen, placing by them rolls of papyrus telling of their happy future, and encasing the bodies in sealed wooden coverings painted with beautiful scenes of bliss, and then laying them away in sepulchres of rock, where they would remain untouched by decay for thousands of years.

Nor does it seem strange that the people of Palestine should go day after day for weeks to the grave to lament. Nor need it seem strange that, in Christian land, the mourner finds solace in going often to the grave, in expending much money to beautify the place with marble, and in decreeing by his last Will that the place shall be kept with everlasting care.

Nevertheless, do as much of this as they may, tend never so carefully the flowers that surround the grave, and preserve with the most anxious care every relic, there is still something wanting, and, unless men can have it, their sorrow goes unsatisfied.

For no Christian will seek the remedy of his sorrow in forgetfulness, in turning away to unworthy pleasures, or to companionships which put out of mind his precious and sacred friends gone before. This cannot be done. What is then the remedy, if such there be? Many have not found it, and have still a void in their hearts. What is that which, receiving, the bereaved can go with no dread to the vacant room; which may not diminish their desire to visit the grave, but will relieve those visits of their agonies of longing?

It is the sweet sense of life continued, of friendship unbroken, of the temporary loss made good by the permanent gain of a spiritual companionship.

There was one who had been out with his dead, and had returned uncomforted to sit by the vacant couch where he so long had watched. But as he sat, he seemed to catch the words,

"'I am here.'
They fell and died upon my ear,
As dew dies on the atmosphere.
Here? Thou art here, Love? 'I am here.'
The echo died upon my ear:
I looked around me — everywhere;
But ah! there was no mortal there!
The moonlight was upon the mart,
And awe and wonder in my heart!

> I saw no form — I only felt
> Heaven's peace upon me as I knelt;
> And knew a soul beatified
> Was at that moment by my side!
> And there was silence in my ear,
> And silence in the atmosphere!"

This is something far removed from that appeal to so-called spiritual manifestations with which some have sought to fill the mournful heart with peace. It is all unsought. It seeks no circle of the credulous for their assistance. It comes in silence, and as uncontrolled by man as the summer breeze; and to make its coming possible, one must enter into the closet in a spirit of prayerful submission to the Divine Will, or read with open heart the pages of the Holy Word.

Of this sense of glorified presence of the loved ones, no one need speak to those who have felt it, and it might almost be said, he cannot speak to those who have felt it not; but from the Lord's example something can be learned about it.

When the Lord said "a little while, and ye shall not see me; and again a little while, and ye shall see me," He spoke of His death. The disciples did not understand, because they were not looking for anything but His worldly triumph; and, when they did understand, sorrow filled their hearts.

But the Lord saw it very differently. He knew that He was about to die, and to die by torture; but He saw the event very much as men see when they stand just without an open door, and look into an inviting room. He could not see death, the door, without seeing beyond it. He could not think of the separation save as being very brief. To Him the new presence after the death was more desirable than the presence before the death, and therefore He felt that they should rejoice when He told them that the death was near. He said, "Do ye enquire among yourselves of that I said, a little while, and ye shall see me; and again a little while, and ye shall not see me; and because I go unto the Father? Verily, verily, I say unto you, that ye shall weep and lament, but the world shall rejoice; and ye shall be sorrowful, but your sorrow shall be turned into joy."

And then He told them of the painfulness of birth-scenes, but reminded them of the rejoicing in which the anguish was forgotten. "Ye now therefore have sorrow. But I will see you again, and your heart shall rejoice, and your joy no man taketh from you."

With the Lord, death was triumph. He had dwelt in an earthly nature for a purpose, and had accomplished it. The temptations which had been met in order to secure man's redemption from evil had been overcome, till there remained only the last and most direful. By means of this He would put aside the earthly, would completely subjugate evil, and would firmly reëstablish the kingdom of God, Himself being the chief corner-stone, and would be one with the Father as the body is one with the soul.

Therefore He would die. Therefore would the apparent triumph of His foes be permitted, since thus captivity would be led captive, and death be swallowed up in victory.

So it proved. The disciples, driven to flight,

did not even have the privilege of burying their dead Master, but hid themselves in fear. All know what followed,—His appearance to Mary, to the two going out to Emmaus, to the eleven gathered in a closed room, and several times more till all sense of loneliness had passed away from them. They did not see Him continuously, they knew that He was no longer as they, but might make Himself visible when and where He would, and then vanish again from sight. By their phrase "in the spirit," which they used, they expressed the truth that they saw Him after His resurrection only when His mercy opened their spiritual eyes. But they saw Him as He promised, and their joy no man could take from them. It sustained them in the most agonizing tortures, and was handed down to those who followed. In what magnificent words Paul says, "For I am persuaded that neither death, nor life, nor angels, nor principalities, nor powers, nor things present, nor things to come, nor height, nor depth, nor any other creature, shall be able to separate us from the love of God, which is in Christ Jesus our Lord." (ROM. viii. 38, 39.)

It is important to call attention to the fact that, after His resurrection, our Lord was not seen by His foes, but only by those who loved Him. "Yet a little while, He said, and the world seeth me no more, but ye see me." The law now was the law of heaven. Those who were spiritually near, and who loved the light, saw Him. Those who were removed in spirit, and who hated Him, saw Him not. It is so in heaven, that they see Him: it is so in hell, that they hide themselves in the caves of the mountains. The angel says "I will set the Lord always before me;" but the evil spirit, if before he deliberately cried, "Away with Him, crucify Him," must now say to the rocks, "Fall on us, and hide us from the face of Him that sitteth on the throne."

The apparent exception of the manifestation to Saul of Tarsus only emphasizes the truth. The Lord did it in mercy. Saul perceived Him, and did not rejoice, but fell fainting, yet his mind was conquered and he became an apostle. Had not the Lord foreseen this, He would not have shown Himself to him.

This truth as to the Lord applies to mortals and to their bereavements. While the Lord's powers and victory transcended those of men, there is the closest possible connection between His experience and theirs. It is only that He went infinitely further in all His experiences.

When the last, slow breath is drawn, and the last answering outbreathing is heard, he who has been sick is asleep. Indeed he had already slept, and already perhaps had murmured in his sleep of those who in the other life awaited him. From this sleep his body never awakes. It smiles from the peace of the spirit which has not yet wholly departed, and by and by loses that smile and all appearance of life forever. A photograph taken in health becomes more full of naturalness than the dead face after the due time has passed.

Meantime, where is the friend? Men make a sad mistake if they think he has gone away, and look up to the stars and think he is there. He is gradually withdrawn from the body, but is not withdrawn from those he loves. He goes to the Heavenly Father, men say; very well, but the Heavenly Father is at hand. He goes to the loved ones gone before; very well, but they are at hand. The Lord had gone to the Father, yet He was by the disciples when they went to Emmaus, and by them when they sat in Jerusalem, and by them when they fished on Galilee. "I am with you always," said He. Again, let the promise be remembered, "The tabernacle of God is with men, and he will dwell with them, and they shall be his people, and God Himself shall be with them, and be their God."

When John in Patmos saw the great multitude which no man could number, did he go? or did they come? No, as soon as he was in the spirit, he beheld them.

The spiritual world is the soul of this world, and is within it as the soul is in the body. Deceased friends do not go into the next room, they are nearer than the next room; and just as near, whether the bereaved remain where they are or remove a thousand miles. They are near when the ways in which they led are followed, and the only distance which can intervene is that which is caused when those still in this life turn away and lower themselves to ways which are opposed to theirs. Then those on earth depart, and not the angelic ones. Then men may lose the sense of their presence, but this is in obedience to the law, "The *world* seeth me no more, but *ye* see me."

Of course they do not stand before the bodily sight, nor speak to the bodily ears, but they are present in all that is essential, and they know the hearts they love and dwell by them, if they are not driven away by worldliness. When the Lord said to the disciples and to all men, that if they kept His commandments, He would come to them and make His abode with them, He spake of Himself, but He uttered the law which governs all spiritual companionship.

If this fact can be understood beforehand, much

will be done to relieve the loneliness of affliction. As men trust God in times of peace in order to lay by a store of trustfulness for times of danger; as they study His Holy Word not only that it may be a light to their ways, but may rise into remembrance when temptations assail; so would they do well to ponder this lesson, for it will surely be needed.

Then, when sickness comes to a loved one, when the precious last days are over, when the final rites are performed, and the mourners return to the silent home, there will still be a comforting thought, something to sustain them as they take up life's duties, a conviction which will enable them calmly to restore the sacred room to its former uses;— and this will be the thought of the near presence, close sympathy and continued watchfulness of the risen friend.

Mention is often made of the contracting circle of near friends, and of the lessening number of the revered aged; is it realized that the unseen, but not unfelt company of risen ones grows larger continually, and awaits in hope and peace the coming of those whom it will receive into everlasting habitations?

If men have any sense of this in their hearts, a season of unusual mortality will not depress so much as it will chasten. It will neither turn any to seek forgetfulness in unworthy ways, nor lead any in weariness to pass their remaining days, lost to all innocent pleasures and taking away happiness from others; but it will make all less eager in life's struggle, less envious of the worldly successful, less inclined to find fault with bodily ailments, and less desirous to be promised a long earthly life.

This cannot be gained, however, without an effort; and, in order to be led to make the effort, the Christian of the New Church must remember his responsibility. The Lord has seen fit to open His Holy Word to him so that he may do it to others. His conduct in this as in all respects is the proof of the worth of what he believes. If he can come peacefully to bury his dead, and if he can return peacefully to his duties, not publicly saying much of those deceased, but not concealing his sense of their continued life, he will do much to lift from the community the gloom which the dark ages produced and hung about death Avoiding not only this gloom but the opposite extreme of hardheartedness, he shall know the meaning of the words," A little while and ye shall not see me, and again a little while and ye shall see me, because I go to the Father." "Your sorrow shall be turned into joy, and your joy no man taketh from you."

www.ingramcontent.com/pod-product-compliance
Lightning Source LLC
Chambersburg PA
CBHW032149160426
43197CB00008B/835